STRESS REDUCTION SIMPLIFIED

BEING HUMAN TO REDUCE STRESS

GURU

ISBN 979-8-89415-219-6

DISCLAIMER

This publication contains the opinions and ideas of its author. It is intended to provide helpful and informative material on the subjects addressed in the publication. It is sold with the understanding that the author and publisher are not engaged in rendering medical, health, or any other kind of personal professional services in the book. The reader should consult his or her medical, health or other competent professional before adapting any of the suggestions in this book or drawing inferences from it. The author and publishers specifically disclaim all responsibility for any liability, loss or risk, personal or otherwise, that is incurred as a consequence, directly or indirectly, of the use and application of any content of this book.

DISCLAIMER

CONTENTS

ACKNOWLEDGEMENTS

I extend my heartfelt gratitude to **Sri Satishji** of Aatmic **Awareness,** my spiritual mentor and guide, whose profound insights and wisdom have been instrumental in shaping this book. His guidance has added immense value and depth to my understanding and perspective. I am also grateful to him for meticulously going through the content, editing and giving suggestions that has contributed in explaining stress reduction concepts in interesting and inspiring way.

I am also grateful to my friend Mrs Geeta Nair, a teacher by profession but a author and poet by heart who gave a perspective on this book from readers point of view and gave valuable suggestion which helped add value this book.

I am grateful to my wife, **Kavita,** a transformational coach par excellence, whose unwavering support and constructive feedback have been invaluable. Her expertise in coaching and her belief in my vision for this book gave me the confidence to bring it to fruition.

I am deeply grateful to my son, **Tushar**, and my daughter, **Trisha,** for their invaluable contributions. Their fresh perspectives from the vantage point of young adults and their thoughtful, mature suggestions have greatly enriched this book. Their input was particularly insightful in identifying the challenges faced by millennials and developing coping mechanisms that resonate with this generation.

I also wish to acknowledge the wisdom and philosophical observations of my dear friends, **Mr Sushil Joshi** and **Mr Govind Agrawal,** whose extensive knowledge and life experience provided profound insight into real-life challenges. Their discussions and reflections have inspired several key ideas in this book.

Finally, my sincere thanks to **Notion Press and my publishers** for their unwavering support and guidance throughout this journey. Their professional expertise and encouragement have been critical in bringing this book to life. To all of you, I am deeply indebted. Thank you for being part of this journey.

MY STORY

After a successful corporate career, I ventured into the small business of specialised printing and trading in printer paper. The business was modestly successful. I was also fortunate to acquire premises for in a struggling industrial area, Lower Parel, Mumbai. I converted this premises into a restaurant close to my factory. This area later became a prime business district of Mumbai after the Textile Mills closed down and, in their place, came High-End Malls and Swanky Office Buildings.

My wife who was working for Garment Export Manufacturing Unit quit her job and started a women wear boutique with a small workshop. Our family was living a comfortable life.

On many days during lunchtime, I used to meet a young executive who was working for a small diamond sorting company located in a nearby industrial estate. We became friends. There was a change in management of the company where my young friend was working, and the estranged son of the owner took over; the new owner was aggressive, ambitious and had big plans for his companies. He tied up with private investors and came out with an

Initial Public Offer (IPO) and raised growth capital from the public. The company ventured into branded jewellery, signed some leading film actresses to represent them as their brand ambassadors, created some well-known brands and started setting up stores all over India and in select cities abroad where the Indian diaspora lived.

They shifted their office from the old industrial estate to a swanky office building in the most expensive business district in Mumbai. My young friend became ally of the young boss to replace long term old employees who were not ready for change and aggressive growth. I followed the company's growth through its advertisements in various newspapers and, in some social conversations, enjoyed dropping the name of my young friend who was in a leadership position in that company. One afternoon, a swanky, chauffer-driven Mercedes stopped in front of my restaurant. My friend had come to meet me; he was telling me all about his newfound wealth, the cars that he had, the homes that he had invested in, his kids were going to international school, and his family vacationed in exotic locations twice a year. After he heard that my wife had quit her job and had started a boutique for contemporary women's wear with a small workshop, he informed me that his company was planning to extend their brands to many products, including women's wear and if we were willing to invest in expanding our production capacities, he would help us in enlisting us as prime vendor for women wear.

He advised me to think big, come out of my comfort zone, set up big ventures and create generational wealth for our kids.

He genuinely wanted me to grow big and put me on to their consultant, who was helping them raise funds from the public and set up their stores. My wife and I set up a Company called Lifestyle Retail Pvt Ltd. We set up two factories to manufacture contemporary women's wear that was being supplied to the stores that were being set up at a furious pace by the brand company. Our consultants advised us to create our own brands and set up some company-run stores in some expensive retail destinations; this would help us get a better valuation from investors as well as create a model that could get scaled up by giving franchises. We got blindsided by the opportunity to earn hundreds of millions by partially offloading some of our shares for a great valuation in the future, and we were already dreaming about luxury cars, luxury homes, foreign education, and destination weddings for our kids.

We invested big money in factories, swanky offices, setting up stores, building brands, proprietary customised software, paid fat fees to the consultants, and hired expensive talent. Like many start-ups ups, we were burning cash, but unlike some other start-ups, we were burning our savings and debts that were being raised by pledging our properties. To earn big money, one had to take big risks. We were supplying our garments to the brand company on a consignment basis; that is, the merchandise was provided for us, and the brand company lent the brand, made available sections in their stores, arranged displays, and did marketing and promotion for fat margin. Our payments would be released only after our goods were sold, their fees and commissions were deducted, we provided merchandise, they provided stores all over India to sell them, and on a smaller scale, we were also setting up our own stores.

One morning, I woke up to a screaming headline in the newspaper that a large public sector bank was scammed by nearly 2 billion dollars by the branded company that had raised money fraudulently. Some months back, the owner purchased citizenship in a country with whom India did not have an extradition treaty, and he, along with his family, was out of the country when a scam broke out. All hell broke loose; the store owners and employees who had not been paid for a few months just looted the merchandise, which included a huge quantity of our goods supplied to the brand company on consignment. The atmosphere was so charged that I narrowly escaped being beaten up physically when I went to a nearby store in Mumbai to retrieve our goods. My friend in that company who I contacted for help was himself in shock; there was not even an iota of suspicion that something was wrong; physical violence had been reported from many stores. The bankers panicked when the scam hit them. They froze our accounts; that is, money could be deposited but couldn't be withdrawn; they were so desperate that they illegally adjusted money which had been deposited in my personal account for remittance to pay college term fees of my son, who was then studying abroad. Fortunately, my friend Mr Govind Agrawal stepped in to pay the fees, or my son may had to discontinue his studies. There was no money to run the operations. The suppliers refused to supply; even the people who were supplying tea and stationery to the office refused to give credit and had to be paid in cash. Key personnel resigned, workers refused to work unless their dues were settled, the owners of the premises where our stores were located demanded that the deposit be doubled, credit card sales, which were being credited to our bank account, being adjusted against the money we owed them and cash sale was being adjusted by employees towards payment due to them. Meanwhile, a Private Bank from which we had taken a loan against our residential property sent a notice demanding repayment of the entire loan amount within 15 days. In our panic situation, we had not been opening the reminders and notices being sent to us; we had missed payment for 90 days, our account was declared NPA and legal action was initiated. Negative remarks were reported on our credit rating, and we were not able to borrow from formal lenders. The bank published an advertisement in the local newspaper, and people started dropping in to inspect our residence; it was a humiliating experience. The stress was so overwhelming that in panic, impulsively, I sold off my factory at a fraction of its real cost to reduce pressure from this lender and take our residence from being taken over by the bank. But the pressure from the company's creditors continued.

I started dreading taking up calls and was so sensitive that I felt that everybody was looking down on me in contempt. My relationship with my family members was suffering. I was constantly irritated and was snapping for no reason. The critical inner voice in me was berating me as a failure, a loser and worthless. My blood pressure shot up, there was an increase in my diabetes level, there was palpitation in my heart, pounding in my head, I could not think straight, my mind was fogged, my head was hurting, and I had acidity issues in my stomach. I could not sleep and woke up in the middle of the night in panic. I consulted a doctor who prescribed medicine for my anxiety, blood pressure, diabetes and acidity. The medicine used to make me drowsy. Therapy was not helpful as I wanted some immediate solutions and was not in a mental state for a long conversation on reframing my negative thoughts. The therapies were also expensive, and I didn't have money for multiple sittings. I was also tempted to have alcohol but, fortunately, could stay away from it. I visited the places of worship for one week; I remember I visited the Buddhist Temple on Monday, the Hindu Temple on Tuesday, the Christian Church on Wednesday, the Jain Derasar on

Thursday, the Muslim Dargah on Friday, the Hanuman Temple on Saturday and the Sikh Gurudwara on Sunday. I was so confused that I wanted divine intervention to get me out of the situation. I climbed 2000 stairs to reach Tirupati. I attended a programme conducted by some Spiritual Guru and tried yoga and meditation; they all gave me temporary relief, but the problem persisted, and my anxiety returned.

One day, while scrolling the internet, I came across the story of Mr Amitabh Bachchan, an Indian Film Super Star who faced a similar experience when his Company, "The Amitabh Bachchan Corporation Ltd., went bankrupt, and he had to personally pay the company debts. He, like me, initially messed up, fighting court cases, declaring his company bankrupt, and ring-fence his personal assets, but the lenders had secured themselves by taking a personal guarantee from him and creating a charge on his personal assets, instead of getting mired in court cases and departmental actions. Mr Bachchan embraced the situation as a challenge, accepted the problem and took up the challenge to pay off his creditors and bounce back. He had no bank balance; his properties had been attached by his bankers; he had no work, nobody was giving him work, and he had debt of nearly 12 million dollars to pay off. The strategy that he adopted of managing his stress, taking action, adjusting, adapting, altering, avoiding, etc., helped him come out of his negative situation in 18 months and altered his career forever. He started doing roles that suited his age, and people loved him in his new role.

I also adopted his strategy; instead of resisting, getting upset, angry, having fear, and anxiety, I embraced the situation as a challenge, accepted the problem and started working out solutions. I took action, spoke to the General Manager of the bank, and told him that we were in a bad situation because of no fault of ours and that we intended to repay our liabilities; the bank also did not want to carry Non-Performing Assets (NPA) in their books and worked out a generous One Time Settlement. I could also have negotiated a maximum home credit loan repayable over a period of 15 years at a very low rate of interest and used that amount to repay the loans of the Company. A calm, honest talk with the General Manager had not only helped reduce the liability but also a way to pay the reduced liability with a loan that was to be repaid over a period of 180 months. We had talked with other unsecured creditors and assured them we would repay in small instalments; understandably, some of them did have some objections, but they realised the offer that we had made was better than trying to recover their money through time-consuming, costly litigation. Even the workmen agreed to similar arrangements; they had so much faith in us that they literally shouted down at the union leader who was trying to create trouble. The GST regime had been launched in India, and the state government announced a generous amnesty scheme, which would allow us to get out of sales tax liabilities. I very easily got out of difficult situations.

By the time I could sort out all the issues and launch a new business, COVID-19 had locked down all business activities. Many people that I spoke to at that time were struggling with fear, anxiety and stress. But I had found solutions to my problems and had got out of the bad situation when I refused to get stressed. My stress took up the challenge of solving my problem and using my intellect to work out intelligent solutions to my problems. The same was also true of Mr Amitabh Bachchan. He could solve his problem after he refused to get stressed by the negative situation, took up the challenge and worked out intelligent solutions. This was not a coincidence. I did some research and found some similar patterns. Shahrukh Khan and his sister Shahnaz Khan grew up facing poverty, hardship, and difficult life situations. After their parents died, Shahnaz was overwhelmed by stress; she went into shock and got depressed. Shahrukh, on the other hand, refused to get stressed, considered the problems to be a challenge to his ability, used his intellect, worked out solutions to his problems and went on to become a big success. A similar pattern was observed in the problems to riches story of Elon Musk and Dhirubhai Ambani. Gautam Adani, Ray Kroc (Macdonald), Col. Sanders (KFC), Walt Disney, Oprah Winfrey, Joanna Rowling (Harry Potter), Jack Ma (Alibaba) etc. This could not be a coincidence; different people, different age groups, and different countries but similar stories; they faced problems in their lives, they refused to get stressed, they considered their problems as challenges to their ability, they used their intellect and worked out solutions which helped become a big success in life.

When I went deeper into the study of this pattern, I soon realised they were being human. Stress is nothing but an animal response; that is, all animals have an instinct to fight or run when they get into a problem and feel threatened. They have fear; they get anxious, upset, angry, aggressive, they get stressed; this is exactly what happens in humans when they get stressed. But this reaction was meant as a survival response; that is, getting stressed helped fight or run from physical threats. But today, humans rarely face physical threats; they face issues situations like issues at work, financial issues, career issues, relationship issues, etc. These are problems, challenges in life, fighting or running away from problems. Getting stressed is a bad response, but people get stressed because it is a survival instinct in all animals. Although many people don't like to believe that humans are also part of the animal kingdom, they will also have this animal instinct. But if we further analyse, we find that humans evolved differently than other animals because they used their intellect to work out solutions to their problems; they analysed, reasoned, did some creative thinking, came out with innovative ideas, experimented and worked out solutions. If we further analyse the challenges that humans face today, we will see that they are not the challenges that were created by nature but challenges that have been created by humans themselves, so reacting like an animal to a problem created by humans will not work. That is, getting stressed by modern problems does not help; what may help is to be sensible and rational, use intelligence (SRI) and work out solutions that are human. People who have succeeded have managed to realise and control their animal instincts, be human, and use their intellect. They considered their problems to be a challenge and worked out solutions.

CHAPTER 1
A DIFFERENT PERSPECTIVE ON STRESS

"Stress is not what happens to us; it is our response to what happens. We can choose our response."

Shahrukh Khan, the Indian movie superstar, lost his mother, Lateef Fatima Khan, in the year 1990 due to diabetes complications; his father, Meer Taj Mohammed Khan, had died earlier. Their family had been struggling with poverty for a long time because his father was not able to establish any business he got into; the regret that Shahrukh Khan still has is that if he had money, he might have been able to give better medical treatment to his parents. Shahrukh's elder sister, Shehnaz Lalarukh Khan, constantly had been stressed due to their family struggle, and when their mother died, she got into shock and depression. Shahrukh refused to get stressed. His family had struggled due to a lack of money, so he took up the challenge to earn big money so that he would never regret not having enough money. He was studying for his master's in mass communication at Delhi University, he left his course and came to Mumbai to get work in films, he had no contacts, no relatives, no experience in films, no accommodation, no money but he was determined, he struggled for nearly two years, he did survival jobs, there were times he had to sleep in a bus shelter and for some good food he would depend on some friends he made. He recalls a temporary job he did as an usher in Gazal Singer, Pankaj Udhas show, where he escorted people to their seats. It is believed Shahrukh got his break in his first film, 'Deewana' because a more established actor who had been signed refused to attend the shoot because the character was negative, and the director cast Shahrukh because he used to hang around the studios every day. What needs to be appreciated here is that Shahrukh was a post-graduate master's candidate; he had no hassle working as an usher, waiter, etc., doing survival jobs, and taking favours from friends like Vivek Vaswani to be put up in their house. The movie Deewana went on to be a Super Duper hit, and Shahrukh got the Best Newcomer award. The lesson from this story is that Shahrukh Khan and his sister, Shehnaz Khan, were similarly educated, similarly intelligent, and faced similar circumstances. Shehnaz allowed stress to overwhelm her, and she got depressed. Shahrukh considered the circumstances to be challenging, but he became determined and worked his way out of the negative situation.

"Stress is like fire; it can burn you, or it can drive you."

Stress, in a very simple word, is a response that is triggered internally in your body in response to pressure or demand that is placed externally. This response includes physical, emotional, mental and behavioural changes. There is more than enough information available on stress, and generally, stress is considered to be bad. But in the case of Shahrukh Khan, the external pressure lit a fire in him, which drove him to be a big success, while in the case of his sister Shahnaz Khan, the fire in her that was lit due to the pressure outside destroyed her. It would be helpful to understand why.

Stress is identified as a survival mechanism; it is present in all animals, including humans, and it helps animals survive threats to their lives. In nature, where there is no rule of law, the pressure an animal can face is a threat from predators animal; fighting or running away from predators helps them survive, so if the animal perceives a threat to its life, the body could get stressed to fight or run to save a life, this is called the fight or flight response. There would be more energy released in the body, and that would be rushed to the parts of the body that required more energy to fight or run, that is, hands, legs, brain, etc. To rush energy, blood pressure had to be increased, and that required an increasing heartbeat, which in turn called for rapid breathing. One could fight or run away to save one's life if there was fear, anxiety, anger, aggression, irritation, etc., so these emotions were added. Feeling sleepy would be a disadvantage, so stress makes it difficult to fall asleep. Survival is a basic instinct, so stress is triggered instinctively when a threat is perceived. It is an involuntary reaction.

Humans evolved differently than other animals because they realised that getting stressed was not helping them; they became sensible and rational and used their intelligence. They considered their problem to be a challenge and worked out solutions to it. While animals react and are still reacting to problems, humans work out solutions to their problems. Today, humans rarely face physical threats created by nature, like being killed by predators, fighting or running from natural disasters, etc. They mostly face problems that are self-created by humans, like work issues, money issues, and issues like bigger flats, bigger cars, better schools, etc. These are not threats to life; that is, this problem will not kill us or hurt us; getting stressed does not help, but humans get stressed by these problems, the reason being that the natural feelings to these problems are negative, people dislike them, feel bad, have fear, get anxious, get angry, upset etc. But these negative feelings are working against them. When humans are threatened by predators, they dislike the situation, feel bad, have fear, get anxious, got a These feelings are connected with the threat by our brain, and our brain has been programmed to activate our body to fight or run, get stressed if it perceives a threat to our body. Our brain does not segregate between threats to life and problems in life. If the brain perceives that we dislike a situation, have fear, get angry, etc., it will naturally feel that we are under threat and would get us stressed. As described earlier, stress can make it difficult for us to work out solutions to our problems. Stress can sometimes overwhelm you.

Mr. V.G. Siddhartha, the coffee tycoon known for his famous brand Café Coffee Day. He became so passionate about growing his brand that he recklessly borrowed in anticipation that the money that may come in from the IPO could be used to reduce debt, but the IPO did not perform as per the plan; the venture capitalist wanted their money back, and his money also got stuck due to external reason, he panicked, considered himself to be a failure and ended his life but before committing suicide if he had calmly thought over or discussed his problem with somebody who was not going through the same pressure, he would have realised that the debts of his company were around 400 million dollars while his personal assets in the form of 15000 acres of coffee gardens and his various investment as a venture capitalist in many companies including Mind Tree Technologies, land holdings in SEZ etc was worth more than 2000 million. He could have easily sold some of his assets and paid off all his debts, but stress did not allow him to think straight. His wife Malavika, who had never managed a business in spite of the tragedy, was calm; she sold off some assets, shut off some stores and is in the process of rebuilding their business.

Stress could be so overwhelming that for some moment it can make people insane and commit an act that could be of lifelong regret, let me share with you the case of

Mrs Deepali Ganore and her son Master Siddhant Ganore, the only child.

Mrs Deepali Ganore, like any mother, wanted the best for her child Siddhant, who was also a quiet, obedient child. Like any middle-class mother, Mrs Deepali also wanted Siddhant to study, get good marks, be an engineer, and get a good job. But as it happens with many teenagers, Siddhant got distracted. Mrs Ganore got upset; she scolded him like any mother and would get furious if he did not score good marks. In the final semester, Siddhant failed; Deepali was furious with him and scolded him. Siddhant was already stressed, and his mother's scolding added to his stress. He was not able to control himself; stress turned him into some kind of animal, and in that moment of insanity, he stabbed his mother and kept on stabbing her like a man possessed. He did not know what he was doing; stress had overwhelmed him. Deepali died of stab wounds; her body was found in a pool of blood, and next to her body, a message was scrawled that said, "Tired of her. Catch me and hang me." This was followed by a smiley emoticon. A family was destroyed because the son was not able to handle pressure, and stress had overwhelmed him.

Let us take the case of Mr Atul Subash, who has shaken up India now; a young techie in a divorce proceeding felt harassed by an alleged misuse of the law. The process and the system felt so overwhelmed by stress and thoughts that there was no easy or early way to get out of the stressful situation, so he committed suicide, but before that, he made a lengthy detailed video about how the law, process and system is being misused and left a detailed suicide note, implicating his wife and the local judiciary which has shaken the conscience of the nation. While on the face of it, there seemed to be no immediate way out of the harassment, but instead of committing suicide, Mr Subash had taken the negative situation as a challenge, used his intellect and tried to work out some solutions, maybe a young achiever's life could have been saved. Among the options he could have considered, he could have consulted people who work in that system to figure out strategies used by others to counter the misuse of the system, or maybe he could have written to the Supreme Court or High Court threatening suicide if he was being harassed by the system and not been given early justice. He could have held a press conference or taken the issue up on social media. Maybe he could have left his job and camped in the town where his case was being heard and countered the case by stating that now he is jobless and his wife is working; she should now support him. There may have been many other possibilities which he could have explored if he had just been able to control his overwhelming emotions and not committed suicide.

Humans are intelligent animals; instead of getting burned down by the fire that gets lit within them by getting stressed, they find a way to use that fire to drive them towards great success. Stress is triggered by the perception of the situation; if our brain automatically perceives a situation to be a threat to our life, it would trigger stress within us, but if we perceive the situation to be a challenge to our ability, our brain could get us all charged up to work out solutions to our problem.

Mr DHIRUBHAI AMBANI's STORY

The founder of the biggest company in India, Reliance Industries Ltd, Mr. Dhirubhai Ambani, when he started his career, was facing a lot of problems at Aden, a port city in the Arabian Peninsula bordering Yemen, which was a British Colony and there were many British Trading Companies located there. Mr Ambani used to work for A. Besse and Co. The Arabs in Yemen led a violent struggle to include Aden in Yemen. They wanted the British and their employees to go back. There was violence, murder and arson; the place had become an unsafe place. His company decided to close business and move out of Aden; they gave their employees the option of relocating to any of their other trading offices, including their office in London. His relatives were tempted to get an opportunity to move to England. Mr Dhirubhai Ambani didn't want to be a second-class citizen anywhere, so he decided to move back to India, but Chorwad in the Junagadh District of Gujarat did not offer many opportunities. He decided to move to Mumbai with his family. The issue at that time was that he could not transfer his bank balance or sell his house and remit the amount. He had to leave everything behind. Mr Ambani was in a difficult situation, with no job, whatever he had saved was all gone, and violence and constant threats. He refused to get distressed, took up as a challenge and moved to Mumbai with 1000 British pounds, which at that time was worth Rs 15000/-. He rented a small apartment in Chawl type building called Jaihind Estate at Bhuleshwar and rented small office at Narshi Natha street Masjid Bunder in partnership with his cousin Champaklal Damani and set up Reliance Commercial Corporation, he started trading in spices and tried his hand in many goods and commodities. His cousin left the partnership because he felt Mr Ambani was taking too much risk, but Mr Ambani had taken a challenge, he was determined, he refused to have any fear or anxiety, and continued his trading till he found his pot of gold in imports of PFY, Polyester Filament Yarn which was used in the making in making fabric, the money that he made in imports enabled him to set up his first mill Reliance Textile which sold in brand name "Only Vimal." Reliance Textile today has become Reliance Industries with interest in PFY manufacturing, Petroleum Refining, Gas Exploration, Jio Telecom, Reliance Retail, etc.. and the 1000 British Pounds invested in the business are today worth more than 100 billion pounds. Mr Ambani succeeded because he did not get overwhelmed by the pressure put on him; he refused to have fear, anxiety, stress, etc. He took up the challenge to succeed.

In the case of Mr Siddhartha, he was in a difficult situation; he felt threatened. There was fear, anxiety, anger, and guilt, and he felt helpless and worthless. He got overwhelmed by distress or bad stress, which may sometimes drive people to commit suicide. Mr Ambani was also in a bad situation, but he felt challenged; he did not have fear, anxiety, or anger; he had confidence in himself. He got charged with eustress or good stress. It was a similar difficult situation, but a change in perception changed their response.

Let us see how this would be applicable to negative situations in modern life. The issues that modern humans face are problems in life like money problem, problems at work, problems at home, etc are problem difficult situations and challenges in life; they are not threats to life; fighting or running away is not the solution; getting stressed would be a wrong response but our natural tendency would be to dislike the situation, feel bad, have fear, get anxious, get angry, get upset etc., This emotions are linked to threat by our brain so our brain would instinctively perceive the situation to be threat and trigger stress that is resistance in our body. This would create a disadvantage because when our body is stressed, it could get tense, there could be irritation, aggression, headache, head fog, it would be difficult to concentrate, there could be constant distraction in the form of negative thoughts, discomfort in the body, stomach upset etc., stress could make it difficult for us to sleep, we may feel restless, we may dread facing the situation and may have tendency to avoid showing up, this all creates disadvantages and in no way addresses the situation but if we don't let our mind decide for us and we decide for the mind, we do not let our mind control us, we control our mind than we can create great advantages for us, say we consider the situation to be a challenge, take up the challenge that we are not going to be stressed by the situation, take up the challenge to find solutions to our problems. The advantages that we create for ourself is that we reduce cortisol, the stress hormones in our body, lower our blood pressure, improve sleep quality, increase energy level, increase confidence, improve mood, increase our ability to rebound, increase sense of control, reduce anxiety and worry. Improve focus and concentration, enhance problem-solving skills, increase creativity, and improve our decision-making ability. There is a proactive approach to challenges, increased motivation, improved overall well-being, better relationships, improved productivity, and a greater sense of purpose and fulfilment.

The following chart will explain to you the change that happens in our body when we allow our brain to perceive a difficult situation to be threat and the change that happens in our body when we interpret a difficult situation to be a challenge.

PHYSICAL CHANGES

THREAT	CHALLENGE
1. High increase in heart rate	1. Mild increase in heart rate
2. High increase in blood pressure	2. Mild increase in blood pressure.
3. Adrenaline release (High)	3. Adrenaline release (Mild)
4. The body gets into Fight or Flight Mode.	4. The body gets into challenge mode.
5. Blood vessel gets constricted	5. Blood vessels are dilated
6. The body gets tense.	6. The body gets charged
7. Fatigue, Discomfort, Difficulty sleeping.	7. Energised, Motivated

EMOTIONAL CHANGES

1. Overwhelming feeling of fear, anxiety, irritation	1. Positive, excitement, determination
2. Consistent worry, low confidence	2. Sense of challenge, high confidence.
3. Urge to fight or run away from the problem.	3. Motivated to face the problem.

MENTAL CHANGES

1. Difficulty concentrating. Racing thoughts.	1. Focused, Goal oriented thinking.
2. Memory problem. Forgetfulness	2. Clarity in thinking. Sharp memory.
3. Mental fog. Rumination.	3. Positive stress. Solutions driven.

BEHAVIOURAL CHANGES

1. Procrastination. Avoidance	1. Determination. Engaged.
2. Disorganised. Impulsive	2. Organised. Controlled.
3. Isolation. Overreaction	3. Connected. Restrained.
4. Erratic. Withdrawn	4. Consistent. Sociable.

By allowing our brain to perceive a difficult situation to be threat we allow our brain to control. By considering the negative situation like a challenge, we are in control of our brain. All animals fight or run, get distressed when they feel threatened by a problem. It is only the humans who considered a problem to be challenge, found solutions to their problem and became humans.

CHAPTER 2
BE HUMAN

"Humans are intelligent, rational animals."

– Aristotle

The genome sequence, done by the National Library of Medicine and many other laboratories worldwide, indicates that humans and chimpanzees shared common ancestors approximately 5-7 million years ago. Nearly 98% of the chimpanzee's DNA matches human DNA. Scientists consider chimpanzees to be the nearest relatives of humans. Despite this close relationship, humans and chimpanzees have evolved differently. Humans have progressed and developed, while chimpanzees still move around naked, jump from tree to tree, and are still being hunted and killed by predators. Why?

Although humans and chimpanzees have many things in common, the major difference is in the size of their brains. The human brain is three times the size of the chimpanzee brain, and the difference is mainly in the upper part of the brain called Neo Cortex, which is bigger and denser. This part of the brain houses our intellect and is responsible for executive functions in humans, like rational thinking, reasoning, analysis, creativity, innovation, problem-solving, language, sharing, etc. The Neo Cortex part of the brain is called 'Neo' (which is 'New' in Latin) because it is believed to have grown subsequently. This part of the brain is called the modern or higher brain, while the older part of the brain is called the primal or lower brain. Sometimes, the upper part of the brain is referred to as the human brain and the lower part as the animal brain because the upper part of the brain is used for rational response, while emotional reactions are triggered from the lower part of the brain. Philosophers call humans rational animals because they were animals who transformed into humans after they became rational.

THE LOWER BRAINS OF CHIMPANZEES AND HUMANS ARE SIMILAR

The proportion of lower brain structures, like the reptilian brain and limbic system, in the lower brain occupy a relatively similar percentage of the total brain volume in humans and chimpanzees.

Brain stem functions, such as breathing, heart rate, and sleep cycle, are proportionately similar.

The limbic system, which includes parts like the amygdala and hippocampus responsible for emotions, memory, basic instinct, emotional processing, fear, anxiety, stress, and avoidance behaviours, is similarly proportioned to the size of the brain in chimpanzees and humans.

The lower brain structure in chimpanzees and humans have the same functions and plays a similar role in handling fundamental processes essential for survival. The lower brain structures of chimpanzees and humans are proportionately similar and perform comparable functions. The major difference between chimpanzees and humans is the size and complexity of the higher brain, which is more developed in humans. The higher brain is known as the intellect part of the brain; therefore, humans are known as intelligent animals.

The lower brain functions are in conflict with the upper brain functions. Lower brain functions are reactive, fast, and geared towards survival, risk avoidance, mistake avoidance, and adventure avoidance; the reactions are automatic and unconscious. The upper brain, on the other hand, is responsive and involves cognitive functions such as reasoning, rational thinking, planning, problem-solving, abstract thought, creativity, self-control, decision-making, and language. However, upper brain responses need to be activated consciously and deliberately. They are not automatic and reactive like the lower brain. Therefore, you have to put in effort to use the upper brain and be human, while the lower brain will react automatically and instinctively. Your automatic reactions would be those of an animal.

The lower brain would trigger an emotional response when it perceives a threat. There would be fear, anger, and aggression, and it can get the body stressed to fight or run away from a situation it perceives to be dangerous. While the higher brain might evaluate the same situation rationally and decide that a different, more measured response is appropriate. The lower brain seeks instant gratification, avoids pain, and follows instinctive desires. The upper brain would forego immediate gratification for long-term benefits. The lower brain prefers habitual behaviour and routine; it works on instincts and impulses. While the higher brain would work on reasoning, rational thinking, and using intelligence.

In stressful situations, the lower brain dominates. It perceives threats and triggers fear, anxiety, anger, and aggression – all helpful emotions that can aid in fighting or running to survive. Stress helps to fight or run. Meanwhile, the higher brain could be slow to respond as it reasons and could be working on strategies to solve the basic problem. In situations that animals face where there could be a threat to life, where you could get physically hurt or killed by the situation, the survival response triggered by the lower brain is helpful.

There could be some situations in modern human life wherein reactions triggered by the lower brain could be very helpful, like being in a physical danger zone, being caught up in a natural disaster, fighting, or running away from predators. However, normally, people don't face physical threats to their lives but may face threats to their lifestyle, such as losing a job, not having money, problems at work or at home, failing at something, setbacks, etc. The responses triggered by the lower brain, like fear, anxiety, anger, aggression, the instinct to fight or run, getting stressed, etc., are inappropriate for modern threats. We tend to react before we respond because the lower brain or our animal brain processes input before it reaches our higher or human brain, and the lower brain is designed to react instinctively without thinking.

WHY DID INTELLECT DEVELOP IN HUMANS?

The theory is that both chimpanzees and humans originated from East Africa. The oldest skull of Homo Sapiens called "Lucy," believed to be 3.2 million years old, was found in Ethiopia. During the prehistoric period, East Africa was a lush green forest, and human life was similar to that of chimpanzees. Later, due to climate change, the green cover dwindled, and most of East Africa was turning into savannah, a grassy plain land with few trees. This created a big problem as the green forest cover was not enough to accommodate both chimpanzees and humans. The chimpanzees retained the forest cover, and the humans were forced to migrate to the plains. This is like if the families get bigger or the house gets smaller, the adventurous are forced to shift out and migrate. But on the plains, the humans became more vulnerable to predators as they did not have the security of trees to escape from predator attacks. So, humans started evolving to the requirements; the initial evolution in humans was that they stood up on their feet, they became tall and could see over the grass, their hands were free for food gathering and fighting, and the predators avoided hunting something that seemed bigger than them. But this was not enough because the predators were stronger, faster, bigger, and more equipped than humans. The survival response of fight or flight, that is, getting stressed, getting angry, upset, being afraid, anxious, fighting, or running away, was not helping; they needed something different to survive. That is when they started thinking, analysing, reasoning, and being creative. They started using the intellect part of the brain to work out solutions to their problems. Like any other muscle, the more humans used their brains, the more their brains grew, and that part that grew was the intellect part of their brains as that was being used to work out solutions to their problems and challenges. This is called the elasticity of the brain.

For example, let us see how humans solved the problem of predators which were chasing and killing them. Humans analysed that the predators were faster, bigger, stronger, getting angry, upset, and stressed. Fight or flight was not helping them. They used their intellect. They reasoned that they could not fight or run away from a predator which was stronger and faster. They reasoned that they had to work out a solution where they could engage with their predator from a distance. Using their brain, they worked out a solution. They started throwing stones. They also worked on strategy, wherein they collaborated and jointly responded to the attack from the predator. Initially, they threw stones, later spears, bows and arrows; nowadays, they use bullets. The predators may have been faster, stronger, bigger, etc. They had an advantage only if there was a physical confrontation, but they had no answer to something that was thrown at them from a distance and no answer when humans cooperated and started hitting the predators from all sides. The predator had not seen or experienced anything like this before. Earlier, helpless prey, which included humans, used to get stressed and react with a fight or flight response without thinking. But intelligent animals, such as humans, started thinking, working out creative solutions, and hitting back at them. Tables turned, the hunters became hunted, and the predators soon learnt not to mess around with this intelligent animal who would hit them back from a distance. The predators started avoiding humans and focused on safer and easier prey, that is, those animals, which included chimpanzees who did not use their intellect, did not work out solutions to their problem, and tried to survive by getting stressed, fighting, or running away from their problem. Since chimps only get stressed, fight or run away when they are still threatened by predators. Humans use their intellect and reason to resolve their problems, so the predators are now threatened by humans.

UNDERSTANDING HUMAN ECOSYSTEM

Humans had discovered their greatest empowerment: the power of their thinking. They used their intellect to find solutions to their problems. They did some creative out-of-the-box thinking. They solved the problem of food by inventing farming, horticulture, animal rearing, fishing, etc. To help cook and keep warm, they invented fire. To aid mobility, they invented wheels. Humans solved each other's problems. They started specialising; some became doctors so that they could take care of others' health, some became soldiers and police so that they could protect others, farmers would grow food, and actors would entertain. This is how the human ecosystem evolved, where people would sell goods and services to each other, and the means of exchange became currency or money. Money could provide for better healthcare, goods, and services, leading to better dwellings, better mates, better food, more respect, rewards, and recognition. This led to competition, expectations, disappointment, failure, setbacks, uncertainty, insecurity, and aspiration. Children were told from an early age that to survive and live a good life, they needed to score good marks, compete, get better jobs, and earn more money, and then they could get better partners, more comforts, recognition, rewards, respect, etc. Threats to well-being in life were introduced. This was a psychological threat, different from the physical threat to life.

Life is unpredictable. The reality may not be as expected. There could be uncertainties and insecurities. Things may not be the way we would like them to be. There could be setbacks, failures, changes in technology, artificial intelligence, redundancy, etc. Negative situations could be created by external factors that are beyond our control. Negative situations can automatically trigger negative thoughts. Negative thoughts could be perceived as a threat, and if a threat is perceived, our brain could stress our body to fight or run from the problem, and that would be the wrong response because stress does not solve modern problems but rather adds to the problems by creating problems in our body. Humans are animals by nature, and like any other animals, they fight or run. The survival response that has been programmed by nature would get automatically triggered, and the stressed body helps to fight or run. However, the problems that modern humans face are not threats to their lives but problems and challenges that may be threats to their lifestyles. The solutions to threats to lifestyle are not stress, fight or run but calm, reason and resolve.

CHALLENGES CREATED BY MODERN ECOSYSTEM

The modern ecosystem has created a new source of stress, which includes: -

- Work-related stress: there are higher demands placed, long working hours, unclear expectations, lack of clarity, uncertainty, job insecurity, and lack of control over work.

- Golden handcuffs. People have to work, whether they like it or not because a salary is required to pay EMI and bills, meet demands from family, and put food on the table.

- Financial stress, the cost of living has increased, inflation is biting, expectations have increased, demands and requirements have increased, there is a mismatch, and that is creating stress.

- Social stress. Society's emphasis on financial success is also putting a lot of pressure and has been affecting relationships and social equations.

- Investors pressure. Modern business has adopted a principle that the purpose of business is to create investors' wealth. Human resources have become expendable; layoffs in the name of cost-cutting and improving efficiency have been creating stress.

- Technological stress: the world is changing at a fast pace, and there is rapid innovation, making it difficult for some people to catch up with technology; obsolescence has increased.

- Distraction has increased with WhatsApp, Facebook, YouTube, Netflix, etc. There is an instant rush of dopamine, leading to digital addiction that is causing stress.

- Lack of sleep has become a big issue, long working hours, long commute, constant state of arousal, social media addiction have disrupted sleep. The body is also not able to repair, rejuvenate, or relax; there is no time for the parasympathetic nervous system to kick in.

- Lack of time to exercise, the increased work demands, pressure, long hours, etc., leave no time to exercise and burn off the stress hormones.

- Unlike early humans who could fight or run when they were stressed, modern humans cannot fight or run as they are civilised and have to control their reactions. They are aroused and restrained at the same time; this is like the accelerator and the brakes being pressed simultaneously, creating a lot of internal friction.

- Comparison, competition, inflation, cost of living, loneliness, lack of social support, environmental issues, pollution, politics, economy, and fear-mongering could cause stress.

WAY TO HANDLE MODERN STRESSOR

The way to handle modern stressors is to be human, that is, respond like a human to deal with modern problems and challenges. Being human is not being animal; the natural response of all animals, including humans, would be to get stressed, fight, or run when they face problems in their lives. This response is triggered instinctively, without thinking. However, humans became humans because they stopped reacting without thinking, thought and worked out solutions to their problems.

Let us analyse the problems that modern humans are facing, be it competition, job pressure, money issues, relationships, health issues, elderly care, etc. Fighting, running away, or getting stressed are not going to solve the problem. On the contrary, getting stressed may harm our health, harm our relationships, create disadvantages for us, etc., and we all know it. However, we still get stressed because this survival response is encoded in the autonomic nervous system and gets triggered when a threat is perceived. Modern problems and challenges may not be a threat to life, but they could be perceived threats to well-being in life. Our brain is coded to trigger stress whenever it perceives a threat and is not able to differentiate between a threat to life and a threat to well-being; it triggers stress without thinking.

Nature, when it designed life, had all living organisms in mind. It created a food chain where the strong eat the weak, and the weak survive by fighting or running away when they perceive a threat. Nature had not figured out that one of its creations, humans, would be outliers. Humans would use their intelligence to work out solutions to problems created by nature as well as problems and challenges created by their intelligence. No animal other than humans faces challenges like job pressure, examinations, money issues, relationship problems, kids' education, etc. These are problems created by human intelligence and require solutions created by human intelligence. Fighting or running away and getting stressed like animals will not solve these problems, but we are going to get stressed because, in nature's ecosystem, humans are animals belonging to the ape family. Therefore, humans will have to learn to control their automatic instincts and consciously use their intellect. As humans, we need to understand and change.

- **Threat to lifestyle is not a threat to life:** Modern humans may face a threat to their lifestyle or well-being, but they rarely face a threat to life. Finding solutions to the problem is required rather than getting stressed about the problem.

- **Reason and response instead of fight or flight:** Modern humans face problems and challenges in life, such as challenges at work, financial issues, failure, setbacks, uncertainty, and insecurity. These issues have a better chance of being solved if you reason and respond. You may not be able to solve your modern challenges by fighting or running away, which can lead to stress.

- **Accept, not resist:** When ancient humans were threatened by predators, they increased their chances of survival by resisting. However, in modern times, if a person loses their job, their likelihood of finding another job increases when they accept the situation and actively search for a new job or alternative income source. Becoming upset, angry, stressed, or depressed will not solve their problem; they need to accept the situation and move on.

- **Adjust rather than refuse to adjust:** When Mr. Bachchan faced a problem, he had no hesitation in adjusting. He requested his son to discontinue his studies, come back home, and start working to support the family. He had no hesitation in doing television shows, which at that time was considered to be a down market because he had no work and had to pay his debts.

- **Adapt rather than refuse to adapt.** People from India went off to Canada or the Gulf and adapted to cold and heat because they got better opportunities. Shop floor engineers adapted to marketing because they found better opportunities. Mr. Ambani adapted to a rented one-room kitchen in the Jaihind Estate Building in Mumbai from his own house in Aden as the circumstances then demanded that. The family later adapted to the most expensive house in the world after they made money. The family still has no hesitation in eating idli and vada sambar from a small eatery at Matunga, Mumbai, while engaging a Michelin Star chef to manage their kitchen.

- **Alter instead of cursing:** In 1981, Mr Gautam Adani managed the small-scale plastic manufacturing unit started by his brother in Ahmedabad. His unit was struggling because of the frequent price increases by polyvinyl chloride (PVC) importers, who were making all the money, but imports were a highly specialised business because, at that time, there was a need for a special licence to import anything in India, the era of Licence Raj. Mr. Gautam Adani knew they would never make money manufacturing, so he studied the import business and established his specialisation in imports and trading. That was his gateway to the global trading business, which led to him setting up huge infrastructure projects and making him one of the richest men in the world.

What changed was that he refused to get stressed by his problem and used his intellect to work out solutions.

- **Change instead of stagnating:** Mr. Azim Premji was stagnating. The family-owned Western India Palm Refined Oil was into manufacturing cooking oil and soaps; the business had stagnated. Mr. Premji, recognising the importance of the emerging IT field, changed the name of the company to WIPRO and entered the high-growth technology sector. Today, Mr Premji is counted among the richest people in India.

- **Avoid job pressure**: Say no when you don't have the bandwidth, avoid toxic people, and avoid provocation, manipulation, and instigation. Avoid provoking people. Avoid financial pressure, create an emergency fund, and avoid credit card loans and personal loans. Avoid getting stressed.

- **Be in control, don't get out of control:** Stress could be triggered automatically by something that you don't like, which is not as per your expectation or when you perceive a threat to your well-being, etc. You may get stressed even before you realise what is triggering stress. The right thing to do is to be in control of stress, emotional arousal, physical arousal, and psychological arousal; behavioural changes may not be good for you. One of the techniques to be in control is to remind you to **"Be Human."** That is when you are aware of symptoms of stress like fear, anxiety, anger, upset, irritation, shallow breathing, increased heart rate, tension building up, headache, discomfort, etc., keep on telling yourself, "Be Human." By telling yourself to be human, you are also indirectly telling yourself "Don't be animal." Stress is a survival response; the animal in you is being activated by your body's defence system to fight or run. This is an animal's response, which is not useful to you in dealing with problems created by humans. You need a human response, and by telling yourself, 'Be Human', you are reminded to reason and respond.

- **If you mind, there is stress; if you don't mind, there is no stress:** There is an interesting story of a top Indian Industrialist whose daughter took fancy to Western pop music and was convinced that her calling was music. Her attire, attitude and behaviour were to match the Western pop culture, which was quite a shock to the conservative community she belonged to. Her mother was quite stressed; she feared her daughter's choice would bring disrepute to the prestigious family. There were constant arguments between mother and daughter, and the daughter felt that the mother was more worried about what others would say than what would bring happiness to her. The father, a very intelligent, worldly-wise man, was calm and cool, and his stand was that his daughter was a very intelligent girl. She is an adult, and she would know what is good for her. If she chooses a career in music, so be it; he always used to say, why should we impose our dream on her? Let her follow what she believes is her passion and her dream. The dream to become a pop star did not work out well; the prodigal daughter returned home. Her father ensured that she got all the space she required. One day, the daughter approached her father with a proposal to set up a microfinance venture that could empower women. Her father made available the money and the support team. Today, her venture is one of the most promising microfinance ventures that is empowering millions of less privileged women to set up their own ventures. She has been recognised among the most promising young business leaders, and she has also been appointed to the board of many companies headed by her father. Her mother did not mind, so there was a lot of stress, friction, conflict and tension in the family. Her father did not mind such a homecoming, and the transition was smooth. She was and still remains the princess who is adored by her father. Mother and daughter have become great friends.

- **Prepare instead of being surprised:** Most of the time, most humans are in routine situations. They do the same work, meet the same set of people, come across similar situations, or there are similar situations in the industry. Stress is the default response, but if there is a prepared response, there could be less stress. For example, we know that in some industries, there could be a layoff. If we are prepared for a layoff, there could be less stress. There may not be regular work in some industries. There could be less stress if we are prepared for the same. People behave in the same way; something provokes them. It would help to be prepared not to provoke or get provoked. The stock market and the economy will always go up or down. There are going to be cycles, and it would help to be prepared for the same so that there could be less stress.

CHALLENGES IN LIFE ARE TEMPORARY

There are more than enough examples of human life where the challenges experienced were transient.

There is a lot of truth in the philosophy, *"This too shall pass."* People generally find solutions to their problems if they do something about it. How many issues that have troubled you in the past are still existing if you have done something about them, hardly any. The problem is people automatically get stressed by what is troubling them, and they don't do anything about what is troubling them, so the stress persists for a longer period of time. Many a time, there may not be solutions for what is troubling them, but getting stressed and harming oneself is not the solution. Accepting, adjusting, adapting, altering, avoiding, etc., could be some of the other solutions.

Challenge Mentality: Many people who have succeeded have used stress to their advantage, including individuals like Mr. Dhirubhai Ambani, Mr. Shahrukh Khan, and Mr Elon Musk. If there is pressure, the body would get charged up; there would be a rush of adrenaline, increased energy, etc. Instead of considering what was putting pressure on them as a threat, that is, instead of resisting feeling bad or getting upset about it, they perceived the negative situations to be a challenge. They had no fear, were not worried, accepted the situation, and went about finding solutions to them. The charge or drive that pressure created helped them. This is called eustress or good stress. However, when there is fear, anxiety, anger, upset, etc., the body considers the situation a threat and resists it, creating all kinds of imbalances within. This is called distress or bad stress, commonly referred to as stress.

Opportunity: While other animals have to find success with limited opportunity, in the human ecosystem, which thrives in serving each other, there are nearly eight billion humans in this world who could have more than eighty billion needs and requirements, giving humans enough options and opportunity to succeed. If a person is not overwhelmed by agitation and emotions and manages to control stress, and if they are calm, use their intellect, and work out solutions, there could be millions of opportunities. There may be many problems that need solutions and many old solutions that would require new and better solutions. *"Jeff Bezos was doing quite well in the D.E Shaw & Co., an investment banking company, but the hours were crazy and pressure was tremendous, money was big, but he had to deliver. The work started affecting his health; it was not worth it. He had researched the internet companies and knew there could be big business opportunities if he could find a way to sell to the consumers directly through the internet. He knew there were billions of people in the world, and all of them required something and bought something. He quit, started his own company, Amazon, and started selling books online from his garage; he used to buy books from local booksellers, and then he started selling many other products. His friends from the investment companies started investing in his business. For the first nine years, Amazon recorded net losses, but Jeff had the conviction that his business model would succeed. It was a numbers game, and there was a huge number of people all over the world. Amazon declared a profit in the tenth year and is making big money, making Mr. Jeff Bezos one of the richest men in the world. Jeff works for eight hours, refuses to get stressed by the billions he loses on products that don't succeed and does not get ecstatic about the billions that he makes on products that do succeed. For him, peace of mind and happiness in life are worth more than his billions.*

Options to fail: If the other animal fails, it could mean losing their life or starving, so they gets stressed, fights, or runs as their existence depends on success. So even if stress is harming their body, that would be a lesser price to pay than not succeeding. But for humans' life does not depend on succeeding every time. What is the maximum that can happen if they don't succeed? They may lose a bit of time, which may be a fraction when compared to their entire life. They may temporarily face a bit of inconvenience, discomfort, and embarrassment in life, which is a smaller price to pay than getting stressed, having diabetes, high blood pressure, stomach ulcers, heart attacks, loss of sleep, etc. Most companies in the world fail more often than they succeed. For Google, one of the world's largest businesses, as of 2022, more than 267 products have failed, while less than thirty have succeeded. The successes have been significant, but they would not have found success if they had not tried, failed, learnt, and succeeded, so they keep on trying. As humans belong to the animal kingdom, they also get automatically stressed if they fail, but there is a difference between human failing and animal failing. If humans fail, there is learning, but if animals fail, it means death; while stressing to avoid death may help animals, stressing, not learning and not moving ahead may harm humans.

Support System: There may be nothing in the world that somebody may not have experienced before, be it a money issue, job issue, family issue, failures, setbacks, etc. You have more than enough resources available for free, such as Google, Chat GPT, etc. Your family, friends, colleagues, and network could be a big source of support. You may find support on LinkedIn, Quora, etc. You can seek support from teachers, mentors, counsellors, and consultants. Altruism is fundamental to human nature because helping and cooperating ensures the survival of the human species. Humans get a different level of happiness if they help others. If you reach out, there may be more than enough people out there who would want to help.

HUMAN SPIRIT

The human spirit is an extraordinary force, the inner strength that is there in every human being that can enable them to cope with problems and challenges in life. Humans can have patience, endurance, and tolerance and wait for the process to deliver. They have resilience, which gives them the ability to bounce back from failures and setbacks, adapt to change, keep going in the face of adversity, and view difficulty as a challenge, an opportunity to grow. Hope enables humans to maintain a positive outlook and expect good things to happen in the future. Hope can provide motivation to keep on striving even when the going is tough. Optimism can foster a proactive approach to problem-solving and develop the will to persevere. Passion, enthusiasm, and love for what one is doing drive an individual to put in effort and time to excel. Maintain determination and commitment to achieve goals despite obstacles. Determined individuals are persistent, resilient, and have patience and endurance. Humans can have a vision of what they want to achieve; they have direction and focus. They can generate inner discipline, which enables them to stay focused and committed to the task even when the going is challenging and tedious. Self-confidence, the belief that they can have in their own ability can enable them to achieve great success. Cooperation and collaboration, as well as shared knowledge and information, are qualities that have made humans thrive.

I HAVE FAILED OVER AND OVER AGAIN IN MY LIFE. THAT IS WHY I SUCCED

In 1978, a 15-year-old boy named Michael Jordan faced a moment that could have crushed many. Trying out for the university basketball team at his high school in Wilmington, North Carolina, USA. He was devasted to find his name missing from the final roster. The coach had deemed it to be too short and not good enough. Standing at 5'10," he was short as per American standards, as the other players were 6'4" or above. What could have been the end of a budding dream became fuel for one of the greatest success stories in sports history.

Jordan didn't wallow in self-pity. Instead, he used the rejection as motivation to outwork everyone around him. Every day, he woke up early to practice, shooting hundreds of free throws and perfecting his form. He stayed on the court long after others had left, practising in solitude. He knew greatness wouldn't come overnight- it required patience and relentless effort. The following year, Jordan returned stronger, faster, and more skilled. His determination earned him a spot on the varsity team; he faced tough opponents, injuries, and moments of self-doubt. Each setback only reinforced his resilience, pushing him to overcome barriers.

Jordan's journey wasn't just about talent. It was about grit and determination. His relentless work ethic continued through college, where he hit the incredible game-winning shot in the NCAA championship; the world was astounded; some said it was a fluke, but the response Jordan had was, "You see the winning shot, *but I see years of practice and thousands of missed shots.*" He was signed by the Chicago Bulls to lead them, but critics doubted his ability, and there was relentless criticism of handing over charge to a young novice. Jordan proved critics wrong; he did not know how to aim to win, and he redefined what it meant to be an athlete. His dedication to training, mental toughness and unyielding spirit led the Bulls to win the National Basketball Association championship six times. For him, hard work and practice were the only ways to win. Along the way, he faced many personal tragedies, including the murder of his father, but every time there was a setback, he returned stronger, with renewed focus and resilience.

THE THREE PROMISES THAT YOU MAKE TO SELF

If you want to stress less, make the following three promises to yourself.

1. I will not be an animal

When you promise to yourself that *"you will not be an animal,"* you are reminding yourself not to succumb to stress-induced emotional, physical, mental, and other instinctual reactions. You are reminding yourself to maintain composure, be rational, stay calm, and not react impulsively or aggressively without thinking. You are reminding yourself to be in control, not to get provoked or instigated, not to commit any rash act, and not to say something that you may regret later. Don't get overwhelmed by fear or anxiety; regulate your emotions, be aware of your instincts, and don't be an animal.

2. I will not hurt myself

When you promise yourself that *"you will not hurt yourself,"* you are committing to yourself that you will not hurt yourself by getting stressed, increasing blood pressure, blood sugar, acid in your stomach, etc. You will not put pressure on your heart and your brain. You will not hurt yourself by losing your sleep, getting angry, upset, irritated, etc. You will not hurt yourself by hurting your family, customers, and colleagues. You will manage your stress response.

3. I will be human

Being human means reasoning and responding, being sensible and rational, and using your intelligence. (Being SRI) Being human means being in control of your reactions and your emotions. Being human means analysing problems, using creative thinking, being rational, seeking support, working out various solutions, and choosing the solution that may be the best in a given situation. Being human also means using human spirit or human qualities like patience, resilience, taking action, adaptation, adjustment, problem-solving, grit, determination, optimism, faith, hope, and enthusiasm.

CHAPTER 3
STRESS REDUCTION FOR MILLENNIALS

"Stress is a choice. So is peace. Choose wisely."

– Anonymous

VIR SHARMA FROM STRESS TO SUCCESS

Vir was the epitome of professional stability during his years with the international bank. He thrived in a culture that championed work-life balance, ethics and a systematic approach to business. But when his vertical was acquired by a target-driven local bank, his world turned upside down.

The new workplace was a nightmare. Targets were sky-high and often unrealistic, cross-selling of unnessacary products was rampant, and business ethics were sidelined for higher margins. The toxic culture bred constant attrition, endless late-night meetings and an ego-driven super boss who believed that long hours equated to productivity. To make things worse, the office relocation increased Vir's commute, leaving him with less time for family and personal rest.

The Breaking Point

Vir's health began to deteriorate. Sleepless nights, constant anxiety, and unrelenting work pressure resulted in high blood pressure, elevated blood sugar, chronic headaches, and stomach issues. His relationship at home suffered, too, once his strong bond with his family was fraying. Yet, Vir couldn't afford to quit. The pay check was essential to support his wife, child, and ageing parents. Desperate for relief, Vir decided to take a few days off and seek guidance from **Guru**, a Stress Support Guide.

The Turning Point

Guru listened intently as Vir poured out his frustrations. Then, with a calm demeanour, Guru explained the root of Vir's stress: **negative thoughts triggering the fight-or-flight response.** "We humans have an animal brain that reacts to threats with fear, stress and instinct," Guru said, "But we also have the gift of a rational mind, which we can use to face challenges intelligently. The problem isn't our situation - it's how our mind perceives it. If we see this as a challenge instead of a threat, our rational brain will take over, and we'll find creative solutions.

Practical Advice for Stress Management

Guru equipped Vir with actionable strategies:

1. **Reframe the Mindset:** Treat problems as challenges. Vir vowed, *"I will not get stressed and fight-or-run like animal. I will be calm, confident, use my intellect and respond like human.*

2. **Journal Writing:** Guru encouraged Vir to jot down his worries and emotions daily to process them better.

3. **Build a Support Network:** Talk to family, friends, or professionals for advice and emotional relief.

4. **Set Boundaries:** Communicate with the boss about unrealistic expectations and disconnect from work-related devices an hour before sleep.

5. **Practice Self Care:** Include exercise, yoga and meditation in his routine. Guru also recommended quick five-minute relaxation exercises during work hours.

6. **Compartmentalise Work and Home:** Leave work stress at the office and cherish family time.

7. **Backup plan:** Work on an alternative career path if the bank's toxic culture persists.

A New Beginning

Following Guru's advice, Vir began journaling his thoughts and discussing his concerns with his wife and parents. His wife decided to take up employment to share financial responsibilities while his parents stepped in to manage household chores and child care. Vir also evaluated his skills and passions through the *ikigai* framework. He realised that helping people secure loans was his forte. With his extensive network of real estate property developers and car dealers, he saw an opportunity to start his own financial distribution business. Vir approached one of his former distributors, who eagerly partnered with him. Soon, Vir's business took off, initially focusing on home and car loans but eventually expanding into insurance and mutual fund distribution.

The Result

Today, Vir runs a thriving financial distribution enterprise. He has regained his health, strengthened his family bonds, and found immense satisfaction in his work. The lessons he learnt about stress control not only transformed his life but also inspired others around him to adopt a healthier approach to challenges. Vir's story is a testament to the power of resilience, a positive mindset and practical stress management. It shows that even in the most challenging circumstances, we can regain control and create a brighter future.

CHALLENGES FACED BY MILLENIALS AND STRATEGIES TO HANDLE THEM

Millennials face unique life challenges due to economic, social and technological shifts. Here are some strategies suggested by "Stress Support Group" to handle them.

Financial Instability: Debts, Housing Issues. Uncertain Job Market. Inadequate Salary.

Strategies: Create a budget to manage expenses effectively, avoid credit card debt, and make regular payments to build credit and reduce interest. Prioritise paying high-interest debts first. Build an emergency fund to reduce financial anxiety. Explore side hustles or freelance opportunities for extra income. Explore opportunities offered by the internet. Invest early in retirement funds. Compound.

Workplace Stress and Burnout: Long working hours. Lack of recognition. Blurred work-life boundaries.

Strategies: Set clear boundaries between work and personal life. Practice self-care, including exercise, meditation, and hobbies. Advocate for self by discussing workload concerns with managers. Explore workplace flexibility like remote work, reduced hours. Consider career change if environment is toxic.

Mental Health Struggle: Anxiety. Depression. Loneliness.

Strategies: Seek professional help or counselling when needed. Don't hesitate to consult a specialist when you are not well physically and do not hesitate to consult a specialist when you are not well mentally. Build a strong support system of friends and family, or join a support group. Practice mindfulness. Write a Journal to express emotions. Change what you are saying to yourself. End your day by writing what you were grateful for on that day. Limit social media use if it causes feelings of inadequacy or stress. Incorporate regular physical activity for mental well-being.

Relationship Challenges: Maintaining relationships and Balancing personal growth.

Strategies: Prioritise open and honest communication in relationship. Don't build up unrealistic expectations. Adapt and adjust. Dedicate quality time to strengthen connections. Focus on self growth to be better partner. Respect and appreciation. Seek counselling if issues remain unresolved.

Rapid Technological Changes: Pressure to stay updated. Reliance on technology.

Strategies: Stay updated with relevant tech skills through online courses like Udemy, Course Era, etc. Use productivity apps and tools to manage time and productivity. Scale up from handling routines to tasks that require the use of intelligence. Take a regular digital detox.

Health and Wellness Concerns: Sedentary lifestyle, Poor eating habits, Lack of time for physical activity.

Strategies: Incorporate small but consistent physical activity. Take regular breaks. Five minutes to do meditation, mindfulness, stretching, etc., will improve relaxation and productivity. Gymming or walking in the afternoon or after office hours. Plan balanced meals to ensure proper nutrition. Schedule achievable fitness goals to stay motivated. Schedule regular health check-ups.

Social Pressures and Expectations: Pressure to achieve milestones like marriage, home ownership and career success by a certain age.

Strategies: Focus on personal timelines rather than societal expectation. Life is not race to win, the most important aspects of life is not about achieving the fastest results or constantly competing with others but rather enjoying the journey, learning from experiences and focusing on personal growth rather than solely striving to be "first" or the best. Celebrate small wins and progress. Reflect on defining personal goals and values.

SOME FACTS ABOUT STRESS

There are going to be problems and challenges in life. It may have nothing to do with you; this could be because of external factors you have no control over. It is not your fault. You may have no control over your situations, but you can, if you want to, control your response.

Negative situations could trigger negative thoughts, and negative thoughts could trigger an automatic negative response. Your autonomic nervous system is programmed to resist negative situations. The amygdala, the fear centre located in the reptilian part of our brain, can automatically trigger a survival response from our body. This means we may automatically experience negative emotions like fear, anxiety, anger, upset, and aggression, and there could be an instinctive urge to fight or run. This can lead to stress, panic attacks, depression, etc. These are survival responses present in all animals, including humans. The reason is that survival is a basic instinct in all animals, and the threat that animals face is being killed by bigger animals; this is how the food chain works. But humans face a different set of challenges that is a threat to their lifestyle, and it requires a different response that is instead of getting stressed, fighting or running away from the problem, the response required is to accept the problem, reason, and resolve it. Instead of reacting emotionally, responding rationally is required. However, we tend to get stressed by modern problems and challenges to our lifestyle because the signals that we send to our brain are the same signals that we send when there is a threat to life. That is, we don't like the problems and challenges that we face; there is resistance, non-acceptance, fear, anxiety, anger, upset, disappointment, frustration, etc. Our lower brain, or the animal brain, connects this signal and threat to life and gets our body stressed so that we can fight or run away from the problem.

By getting stressed, fighting, or running away like an animal, you are not solving the problem; you are harming your health, and you may also reduce your ability to find solutions to your problem. Stress can make you tense; there could be headaches; shallow breathing may reduce oxygen being supplied to vital organs; there could be head fog; you may find it difficult to think clearly, focus, and concentrate; you may find it difficult to sleep which creates an additional set of problems, and then there is also the issue of triple trouble. That is, anger, irritation, and the urge to fight triggered by stress may lead to arguments, friction at home, the office, etc. People may not remember the situation, but they don't forget what somebody has told them or made them feel. The situations may get solved after some time, but the crack in the relationship does not heal that fast and can be triple trouble; that is, your problem is not solved, your health is harmed, and your relationship has soured. People also bring on triple trouble when they get into escapism with stimulants like nicotine, suppressants like alcohol, or mood alteration drugs; this becomes addictive without finding solutions to your problem.

Think about it: what is the maximum that can happen? Say you lose your job or fail at something. There may be some discomfort, inconvenience, hardship, embarrassment, etc. There are studies that find that most of the issues are temporary. This does pass. 97% of the time, the issues that make us anxious do not happen, and if they do, we easily solve them. Suppose you are calm, composed and aware. You can control the animal instincts that are automatically triggered in you, respond like a human that uses your intellect, and work out solutions. The chances are that you may easily get over your challenges.

RITA - "LIVE IN THE MOMENT GIRL"

Rita had always been a "live in the moment" kind of person. She worked hard at her job and spent on things that made her happy, for her life was about experiences; she loved to travel, and her holidays that year included a week on the Amalfi coast in Italy and a day holiday in Budapest and Prague. She never gave much thought to saving. Life seemed fine-until the day it wasn't.

In the early hours of Sunday, Rita's mother woke up wheezing; her blood pressure had gone to an extreme level, and she was not able to get up. The previous week, her mother had been suffering from a fever, and she had been receiving treatment from a General practitioner, but that night, her condition worsened. Rita called for an ambulance and rushed her mother to the nearest private hospital. Some emergency treatment was given in the emergency room, and the doctors advised that her mother was to be shifted to ICU. Her mother was taken to ICU, and the hospital informed her to deposit One lakh rupees. The hospital did not have a cashless facility; she had to deposit money and then recover from the insurance. Rita had multiple credit cards, but all of them had maxed out. Desperate, she turned to her own friends and family, but they had their own story of struggle. The friends who turned up at the hospital were like her; they had no savings, and their cards were maxed out. They had no credit because nobody was willing to help them. Rita started crying; fortunately for her, the senior doctor in the ICU did not even know her, sympathised and paid a mandatory deposit in the hospital. The next day, Rita desperately tried to raise some funds, but her credit rating was bad, and most of the banks refused to lend. Finally, she raised money from a local money lender at a Mafia rate of interest by depositing property documents of her house; she had not been able to raise money from the bank against that document because the house was in the joint name of her mother and herself, her mother was not in a position to sign. Fortunately, her mother recovered, but Rita could only recover 70% of her expenses from the insurance company as she had not read the conditions. She had to pay the principal along with heavy interest to the local money lender. Rita learnt her lesson; she has changed her philosophy.

A LIFE LESS STRESSFUL

Build an emergency fund. The main cause of stress is money. You fear losing your job because you need money. You have bills to pay, and you feel pressure because of money. You are afraid to quit because of financial needs. Many times, issues in marriage are about money. Hardly anything cannot be solved in about a year, but you need money to survive. First, save, then spend. Money in the bank gives you courage and confidence and makes you less insecure, uncertain, and less stressed. Avoid debt. Many times, in an expensive housing market with high-interest rate conditions, it makes sense to rent rather than buy because the rental cost may be much less than the interest cost. You always have the flexibility to move where there are opportunities. The same applies to high-end expensive cars; their value depreciates. Making statements on a weak foundation may not be advisable. Some of the wealthiest people in the world move around in regular cars, including Mr. Warren Buffet and Mr. Azim Premji. A wedding is another expense, where people let their emotions rule over their common sense and want to make a statement to impress others. There are more than enough cases of people going overboard on their wedding expenses and then paying debts for a lifetime. It makes sense to secure the future rather than impress guests. A minimalistic lifestyle is also advisable. Employment has changed; there is no lifetime employment guarantee. If you add value, the employer wants you. If you are not adding value, you may become dispensable. What value you are adding should be a regular question. There is a need to invest time and money in increasing your value proposition; learning is continuous. Debt instruments charging usurious interest rates, like rolling over credit card debt and personal loans at high interest rates, may perpetually keep a person in debt, and the collection tactics employed by the collecting agency are a source of high stress and disturb the peace of mind. Unfortunately, medical expenses can drive a person to poverty. Adequate medical insurance is a must, as is low-cost term insurance, so that the family does not have to struggle with debts if the main earning member loses their life. Whether we like it or not, life is unpredictable, death is a reality, and time is a resource that is not replaceable. This realisation may help us change our perspective on life.

DON'T FEEL BAD

"Don't Feel Bad" is a conscious effort to break away from automatic stress responses triggered by negative situations and instead approach problems with a deliberate, calm, and solution-focused mindset. Stress often stems from **negative feelings** (fear, anger, sadness) triggered by **negative situations** (work issues, money problems, relationship challenges, etc.) These feelings **trigger stress** and activate the body's fight or flight response, which was crucial for the survival of early humans but is often unhelpful for modern, non-life-threatening challenges.

Stress-related reactions like increased heart rate, elevated blood pressure or digestive issues do not solve problems like job loss, financial difficulties. Reacting to stress **does not contribute to solutions;** instead, it often worsens health and emotional well-being.

The solution lies in a **paradigm shift** - moving **from automatic responses to intentional, thoughtful actions.** Instead of seeing challenges as threats, they can be seen as challenges to be human, to be "sensible, rational, intelligent." (SRI), reason, and respond. This will involve

1. **Acceptance:** Acknowledge the problem without resistance or denial.

2. **Rational Thinking: Use** logic to analyse the situation calmly. Ask: "What **is the actual issue? What can I do about it? What are possible solutions?**

3. **Focus on solutions:** Shift energy from emotional reactions (anger, fear) to practical actions.

4. **Sensible, Rational, Intelligent (SRI) Approach:** Be calm, act (solve the problem) or adjust, adapt, alter, avoid, leave it to God to find the answer. Develop patience, resilience and sense of determination.

5. **Intentional Living:** Operate in a deliberate mode where responses are conscious and purposeful rather than automatic and impulsive.

Elevate self, visualise self as a **higher human being, (SRI)** a person who is sensible, rational, intelligent, who would not get stressed, fight or flight like an animal when there are challenges but remain calm and composed, reason and respond to a negative situation. Consider each problem to be a test of being human, which tests your ability to work out solutions, adjust, adapt, and have patience, perseverance, resilience, grit and determination. Practical Example: If you lose your job, instead of reacting with fear or despair, break the cycle and have a paradigm shift in your response. Accept the situation, Shouganai, Ukeireru, which is the Japanese word for "what it is, it is. Accept. This has happened; I can't change the situation by getting stressed or beating myself. Analyse options: What are my skills and experience? What value can I add, and what difference can I make? What can I do? Who should I reach out to? How can I find my new income sources? Take calm, deliberate action, do research, meet people, update your resume, network, reach out, apply for jobs or consider learning new skills.

The habit of feeling bad, having fear, anger, etc. Getting stressed, fight or flight response, being an animal, has been there for a long time; it is like you have been eating with your right hand all your life, and now you are being asked to use your left hand; the change will be gradual. "Don't feel bad "does not mean ignoring emotions or pretending everything is fine. It means being aware and acknowledging feelings but not letting them control your response. By reframing problems, paradigm shifts in response, focusing on solutions and responding with intelligence and patience, you can reduce stress and navigate life more effectively.

REDUCE NEGATIVE MENTAL CHATTER

A thing that we have to live within human life is constant thoughts. These are known as mental chatter. When something happens in your life that you don't like, there will be negative mental chatter. You may be saying something to yourself that you may not even say to your enemy. You are saying it because that is a habit that has automatically evolved from the early stages of evolution as negative self-talk helped in staying out of trouble. Today, the situation has changed. You can't stay out of trouble; there are going to be challenges at work, at home, with money, with people, etc., and you would need to use your intellect to deal with these challenges. If you are having automatic negative thoughts, there could be negative perceptions, negative emotions, negative feelings, and naturally automatic negative reactions triggered by these thoughts. If you are reacting negatively, then it is difficult to work out a positive response as stress overwhelms you.

There is a need to reduce the habit of negative mental chatter.

You can reduce negative mental chatter by:

1. Write down your thoughts in a diary, delete thoughts that are negative, unhelpful, or thoughts that put you down, creating a disadvantage, etc.

2. Mindfulness is a good practice to reduce negative chatter. You can close your eyes, be mindful - that is, be aware of thoughts that are being triggered in your mind, observe, be a witness, don't be judgemental, don't react. You would come to know your thought pattern and make corrections.

3. Being SRI, that is, being sensible, rational, and intelligent, can reduce negative mental chatter. Think about any negative situations that you can be in, be it issues at work, at home, with people, with family, with life, etc. Having negative thoughts, feeling negative, being angry, getting upset, getting irritated, having arguments, feeling depressed, etc., is not going to help you. What may help is being sensible and rational, using intelligence, and working out solutions. Remind yourself to Be Sri.

4. Cognitive Behaviour Therapy, which involves challenging and reframing thoughts, is a good technique to reduce mental chatter. A balanced perspective helps.

5. Breaking the spiral of thoughts is also a good technique. The incessant thoughts are being created by neurons in our brains firing and connecting with each other. The more it connects with negative thoughts, the more negative thoughts it creates. You can break the spiral or create a vacuum by mantra meditation. That is, you can sit at some place, close your eyes, and chant *'quiet'* as you breathe in, and chant 'relax' as you breathe out. You can replace the words "quiet, relax" with any word of your choice. The words are not important; what is happening is that when you are chanting, you are not allowing your mind to have automatic negative thoughts, and you are breaking the cycle.

6. Deliberate positive thoughts. You can deliberately have positive thoughts by setting positive intentions, affirmations, positive self-talk, gratitude, support groups, counselling, talk therapy, etc.

7. Keeping busy can help you reduce negative mental chatter. The biggest realisation about stress is that your mind can only do one thing at a time. Even when multitasking, it switches on and off between tasks. If you are having positive thoughts at the same time, you cannot have negative thoughts. By making yourself busy, you are distracting yourself from negative thoughts and focusing your attention

on positive, busy actions. When you are not doing anything, your body may be at rest, but your mind is in full action, having negative thoughts. Make yourself busy and have a busy schedule.

WHAT CAN HELP YOU IN A NEGATIVE SITUATION

Be aware of the stress reactions. There are classic symptoms of stress that are easily identifiable, and there are some simple techniques to defuse stress. Some of them have been shared in this book; learn and practice them to keep your stress response under control.

Stress symptoms are alerts; your mind is perceiving danger. Identify what is bothering the mind.

Remember fear, anxiety, anger, upset, aggression, nervousness, etc., that are getting triggered within you because your brain feels that you are being attacked by a predator. Tell your brain it is not true; there is nothing to worry about, just some temporary challenges. Control your instinct, activate your intellect, analyse the problem, be sensible and rational, use your intelligence and reason, and work out solutions.

There is a negative situation. It is natural for you to resist, dislike the situation, get upset, be disappointed and frustrated, etc., but these are the same reactions that trigger the body to fight or run. Remember, the negative situation is due to external factors. It may not be your fault; it is not in your control, and the situation is already putting pressure on you. Why put on more pressure by resisting, not liking, getting upset, being afraid, anxious, etc.? Although you may not feel like it, it helps to be contrarian. It helps to accept the situation and consider it to be a challenge. Your ability to be human is being tested. Instead of getting stressed, be calm, reason, and respond.

Take support. There is a lot of help available out there. Reach out to your connections, family, friends, consultants, counsellors, network, etc.

Assess your financial situation and budget, cut down on non-essential items, and reduce expenses.

Take care of yourself, exercise, metabolise cortisol, the stress hormone that is being built your body. Yoga and meditation would also be of good help.

Maintain a routine, workout schedule, and get busy.

Manage thoughts, delete useless thoughts, reframe useful and negative thoughts, add or replace with the thoughts that makes you feel good, increase your confidence, and self-esteem.

Maintaining sleep hygiene can help.

Remember, a negative situation in life is temporary. This, too, shall pass. Accept and move on. Don't create more permanent problems for your health by overthinking.

Balance, if there is a problem going on in your life, that does not mean that you can't meet your friends, share a good laugh, watch a movie, play a game, go for a long walk, enjoy a good meal, sing, dance, read, paint, draw, and enjoy. Balancing what makes you happy along with a challenge helps in dealing with the challenge.

If you don't know what to do, do something that you are passionate about, you have an interest in it, have the skill and the qualification for it, it is required by people, they are willing to pay for it, and you are good at doing it. That 'it' is your ikigai, and people who are doing 'it' enjoy and succeed in what they are doing. Doing something activates the reticular system in our brain. The reticular activating system is a network of neurons in our brain that activates the cerebral cortex and maintains consciousness. It works like a powerful artificial intelligence and stops after finding what we seek.

MENTAL HEALTH

Millennials today face significant economic challenges. There are demands and pressure for money. Maintaining a decent lifestyle has become expensive. Housing and schooling costs have become **increasingly** expensive. The job market has become unstable. Pressure at work has increased. There could be insecurity and uncertainty. It becomes difficult to manage work-life balance with the demands and pressures of work. WhatsApp and emails have also become issues as the person is available 24/7. Social media has also added pressure on people to post carefree, happy lives, which may not be true but could lead to comparison and unrealistic expectations. Many celebrities sharing their mental health struggles has created a situation wherein some people feel it is okay to be depressed.

It is not okay to be depressed. It can affect your work, family, and social life. Feeling sad, hopeless, or worthless, being irritated or angry, having low self-esteem, lacking confidence, or experiencing difficulty concentrating could lead to job issues, relationship problems, and financial difficulties. People may have suicidal tendencies when they feel depressed.

Reduce Mental Health Issues

1. Identify what is creating mental pressure. If there are financial pressures, work out solutions to reduce expenses or increase income. If needed, consult a financial expert. Accept reality, don't pretend, and don't spend on something that you can't afford. Debt creates a lot of pressure. If your job is putting pressure on you, work out ways to reduce it. Resistance creates more pressure; acceptance can reduce it. If the pressure from your job is beyond an acceptable level, consider changing your job. Research from Stanford University

suggests that productivity peaks at around 49 hours per week and then declines. Studies suggest that the productivity of workers who work more than 50 hours is less than that of workers who work less than 48 hours per week. Billionaires who suggest working 80 hours per week may be interested in increasing their wealth at the expense of employees' mental health. Sleep is important for increasing productivity. Although the sleep requirement varies among individuals, studies suggest a minimum of 7 to 8 hours of sleep is needed for our brains to rejuvenate and for the body to repair itself. Close shop, switch off messaging services and email after your deadline. If you are not well-rested, you can make mistakes, affecting your productivity, which could be detrimental to your work life. Be sensible, be rational, use your intelligence, and don't be influenced by others.

2. Be human, sensible, rational, and intelligent. Don't compound your problem. For example, if you are facing financial challenges, the reactions that are being triggered in you would be to get angry, upset, irritated, or get aggressive, etc. But if we get angry or upset with our boss, spouse, or family, you may add to your problem. Impulsive action could create long-term regret. People may not remember the problem, but people don't forget how you made them feel. Don't be upset with yourself, don't criticise

yourself and don't put yourself down. By blaming yourself, you are triggering negative thoughts, which could lead to stress and add to your problem.

The issues that you are facing in life could be temporary, but the problems that you can create for yourself could be more permanent. Animal instinct would be a bad habit in us, but as humans, we can control our bad habits and change our responses. It is natural for us to get upset when there is a problem, but the problem that we are facing is not natural. There are no layoffs, money problems, family issues, targets, or deadlines in the natural ecosystem; these challenges are created by humans in the human ecosystem. A natural reaction is a wrong response to a modern problem, but natural reactions would be instinctively triggered. We can be inspired by spirituality, which says the challenges you face in life are a test of human spirits or a spiritual test. The challenges will trigger the animal in you; being human is to control the animal. Instead of resisting, fighting, or running, accept, reason, and respond. Reminding yourself to be human, sensible, rational, and intelligent may help you deal with the problems you are facing.

3. Talk to someone you trust. It becomes difficult to be sensible and rational and use your intelligence when you are under mental pressure. Your mind could generate a lot of negative thoughts, which could trigger

stress, and that could arouse your body, making you restless and nervous. Do talk to somebody that you can trust. It is good to have a confidante, a mentor. Talking to counsellors and therapists is a big help. Create a support system; be in touch with your friends and family. Do talk to your spouse, parents, and immediate family; their support is a big help. Share your feelings. Writing is a big help; maintain a journal. God can be a big help. Do talk to God as you would talk to a good friend.

4. Manage stress. There are many techniques that can be used to manage stress, and a list of some stress reduction techniques has been shared in this book. Check which one works for you.

5. Be good to yourself. You are going through mental pressure, so don't add more pressure by negative self-talk and stress. Regular physical activity is important to metabolise cortisol, the stress hormone. Keep yourself busy, create a schedule and a process, and focus on taking small steps to solve the problem. Work is one of the biggest stress busters as your attention is focused outside, and you are not engaging in negative thinking. As they say, an empty mind is the devil's workshop. Stress is triggered by thoughts, and you have more thoughts when your attention is focused on yourself. Sleep is a great stress buster; it repairs and rejuvenates, so ensure adequate sleep. Meditation

and Mindfulness are not only good stress busters but also give you a great feeling. Like anything new, it may appear difficult at first, but once you practice, you will find it simple. The feel-good chemical dopamine that gets released makes you want to practice every time.

6. Expectation. One of the big reasons for stress is the gap between expectation and reality. Life is under no obligation to make things work out as per our expectations. The reality could fall short of our expectations, leading to disappointment, frustration, and upsets that add to our stress. Many factors in life are not in our control. Life can be unpredictable; there may be surprises, uncertainty, and insecurity. There could be problems, challenges, failures, and setbacks. There can be success and progress; they are all part and parcel of life. As spirituality says, the purpose of life is to have evenness of mind in all moments, disregarding the temporary situation of success and failure.

7. Learning to say NO! is important to maintain your mental health. It prevents overcommitment, limits yourself to the bandwidth available, protects personal time, maintains boundaries, and reduces stress by not overloading yourself. This improves productivity as you can concentrate on manageable tasks, leading to a sense of accomplishment and satisfaction, and boosts your confidence and self-esteem.

When we go through a difficult situation, the chemical changes in our body can put us in a low mood. We may procrastinate, feel like avoiding people, or have cravings for alcohol, cigarettes, or drugs. This is again because of stress, which triggers avoidance and escapism. Say **NO** to low mood, procrastination, avoiding people, and the urge to consume drugs, alcohol, cigarettes, or any other stimulators.

8. Balance negative with positive. A negative situation puts pressure on you and your family. The more you brood, the more irritable you would get. Balance negative pressure with enjoyable activities. Pursue hobbies and interests, take time off for leisure and entertainment, and spend quality time with family and friends. A negative spiral of thoughts would take you deeper into stress. It's important to unwind and destress.

9. Manage thoughts, challenge negative thoughts, replace negative thoughts, delete, and don't pay attention to the thoughts that are not useful. Negative thoughts that make you alert or cautious could be useful. Irrelevant thoughts that occupy your mind space could not be useful. Set intentions, use affirmations, have a positive attitude, practice gratitude, and maintain a journal.

10. Consulting a doctor when we are not feeling physically well is quite common. There is a very high chance that the physical ailment that we are suffering could be because of stress. Survival is a basic instinct in all animals, including humans, and if a threat to survival is perceived, our minds may go out of control. There could be obsessive thoughts, fear, anxiety, ADHD issues, depressed feelings, anger issues, stress etc, etc. Like any physical health problem, there can be mental health problems, and like there are therapists and doctors for physical health, there are therapists and doctors for mental health. An external virus or bacteria entering your body can create an imbalance in your body, and so can negative thoughts about negative external situations. There are doctors who help you with viruses and bacteria; similarly, there are doctors who can help you deal with negative thoughts and depressive feelings. There is nothing to feel shy about taking treatment for mental health issues. It is not a taboo. Mental health challenges are widely prevalent, and some of the most successful people are benefitting by taking mental health treatments.

MONEY PROBLEM

As per the American Psychological Association (APA), 70% of Americans feel stressed about money. Job loss, cost-cutting, rising expenses, focus on investor value, inflation, etc., have added to money worries. Financial problems are one of the most significant sources of stress in modern life. Money is intertwined with nearly every aspect of daily living - housing, food, education, healthcare, and recreation. When financial difficulties arise, they can create a ripple effect that impacts not only one's emotional well-being but also physical health and relationships.

Money problems, if not handled tactfully, can trigger stress that could affect mental health, impact sleep, and reduce confidence, self-esteem, energy, and problem-solving ability. Money problems can generate automatic negative thoughts, which could trigger stress. Stress can impair rational thinking, problem-solving, and decision-making. There is a problem; getting emotional about the problem, getting anxious, getting angry, upset, and having fear is not going to help you solve the problem. Your automatic reaction would be to get emotional, which will create a disadvantage in dealing with the problem; your deliberate effort should be not to get stressed, be sensible and rational, and use your intelligence to work out solutions; in short, control your animal instinct and be human.

Accepting the problem reduces resistance and thus reduces stress. Getting stressed does not help but complicates the issue and impairs our ability to handle it.

Be mindful of your finances, track expenses, and find out where the money is flowing out. Reduce your expenses to only needs, cut out wants, and increase your financial runway. Money problems can be overwhelming; it is always better to build an emergency fund to take care of emergencies that can hit you at any time. Most experts agree that you should first set aside ten percent for compulsory saving, and the balance of ninety percent can then be allocated for expenses and investment. If you spend all your money on wants, you may not have money for your needs.

It would help to talk about your challenges with someone who is not going through the same emotional pressure as you. Just by talking without emotions weighing you down, you may bring about some clarity and a new perspective on the issue you are facing. Keeping the problem to yourself amplifies the same and makes it intimidating. Just ensure the person you are sharing with is sensible, rational, intelligent, and non-judgemental. Open up to your family. They need to know what is happening in your life. They would be more tolerant, understanding, and supportive. It is understandable that they would have their concerns, but communication strengthens relationships. Network, mark your presence in industry meet-ups, call up, seek advice, counselling, consult. If required, talk to a mental health professional. It's okay to not feel mentally well.

Stop the blame game. The challenges in life may not be your fault; they may be because of external factors. You may be a victim of circumstances that are not in your control. You are already in a difficult situation; don't add to your difficulty by making it hard for your mind to think and work out solutions. Also, understand that when you feel threatened, your animal brain perceives that you are being attacked by a bigger animal, so it wants to avoid coming out of the cave and facing the predator. This reduces feel-good brain chemicals like serotonin, dopamine, etc., which can affect your mood and motivation. This is where your self-discipline comes in: *"Do what you fear, and the fear disappears," and "Courage is not the absence of fear but triumphs over it."* Do not avoid calls. Do not fear opening letters or emails. When you face fear, fear crumbles. Ignoring bank and credit card statements can hurt your credit rating, and defaulting can make other lenders avoid lending to you. **Honestly, my financial loss and stress could have been much lower if I had not tried to play smart with my lenders and had not attempted to buy time by trying to buy time by engaging the bankers legally. The banks work like cartels; they share information through CIBIL and other Credit agencies; if there is a delay in payment to one bank and if they declare the person borrowing as NPA, then it is difficult to borrow from others, and it becomes difficult to carry on a relationship. The banks suddenly apply brakes,**

and your business and finances go off the rail. The courts and regulators take time; we had to sell our assets in distress to wriggle out of the chokehold.

It helps to talk to your creditors; they can sense danger. If you tell them about your difficulties, they may find ways to help you get out of trouble. Problems and challenges in life are temporary, and there are solutions. It may be tough, but it is important that you control your natural instinct despite the pressure, be sensible and rational, and use your brain to work out solutions.

Stress creates tunnel vision; it becomes difficult to explore possibilities beyond your limited vision. Money is what you get in exchange for goods or service you give. You have the talent, skill, experience, exposure, education, information, and opportunities. There are nearly eight billion people in this world, and they offer more than two hundred billion opportunities for people who use their intelligence. Allow me to share story of Kris.

STORY OF KRIS

In Mumbai, amidst the chaos of rising rents, job insecurities, and inflation, Kris, an average Indian struggling with money problems, lived. Like 70% of the population, Kris often found himself stressed about finance. A recent job loss had amplified his worries, and with every passing day, unpaid bills and mounting expenses loomed large in his mind.

Kris's sleepless nights were filled with thoughts of failure. He felt his confidence eroding and cloud of negativity seem to follow him everywhere. The started affecting his relationship and productivity. He avoided phone calls, ignored letters and dreaded checking his emails.

On the advice of a friend, Kris met a Stress Support Guide (SSG), and one of his advice stuck a chord. "When *faced with a problem, you would have fear and negative emotions, but fear, negative emotions, stress, fight or flight response are animal reactions meant to address problems faced by animals; you are human, and problems faced by humans are created by humans, animal don't face money problem so reacting like an animal will not solve a problem created by human intelligence. To solve your problem, you need to be sensible and rational, use your intelligence, and respond like a human.*" Taking these words to heart, Kris decided to face his problems head-on.

1. Acceptance: - Kris began by acknowledging his situation without judgement. He reminded self that money problems weren't unique to him and was result of external situation, he had to fix the roof that is either get a new job or find way to make money, Getting stressed was not going to solve his

problem. This simple act of acceptance helped ease the resistance within him, reducing his stress.

2. Understanding the numbers: Kris reviewed his finances. He tracked every expense, identified unnecessary spending, and realised that his love for online shopping was draining his savings. He resolved to distinguish between his needs and wants, cutting out wants to increase his financial runway.

3. Building a Buffer: - Determined to build an emergency fund. Kris committed to save minimum 10% of any income he earned. He reallocated his budget, ensuring his essential expenses fit within remaining 90%. This gave him sense of control over his finances boosting his confidence.

4. Seeking Support: - Instead of bottling up his emotions, Kris shared his struggles with his family. To his surprise, they responded with empathy and understanding. Their support became pillar of strength. Kris also regularly spoke with Stress Support Guide whose objective perspective brought new clarity to his situation.

5. Facing the fear: - Kris mustered the courage to call his bank. Explaining his situation, he found the relationship manager more understanding than he had expected. They offered solutions,

including restructuring his loan payments. By confronting his fears, Kris realised his imagination was much worse than reality. Stress had made him a frightened animal.

6. Staying Resilient: Kris disciplined self to open email, answer calls, maintain calm, address problem, no matter how intimidated he felt. One of the calls was from a recruiting consultant who had been desperately trying to reach out with a better position with better pay., avoidance had unnecessarily made Kris struggle with his problem and stress.

LIKE WHAT YOU DO

In the recent past, I have met many people who don't like what they do. The pressure in the job has increased; there is no time to do what you would like to do. Work-life balance has gone for a toss; they are doing what they are doing because they need the pay check. The EMI and bills have to be paid. There are demands, requirements, and responsibilities placed by society which creates golden handcuffs.

Not liking what you do creates resentment. There is resistance within your body which triggers stress. There could be physical health problems like high blood pressure, diabetes, acidity issues, headaches, sleep problems, tension, etc. There may be anxiety and anger issues; people tend to get short-tempered, which may affect relationships. There is no enthusiasm, reduced motivation, and low productivity, making it difficult to work effectively.

There may be millions who may like to do what you don't like to do. They would love your pay check. Your employers pay you for the value that you add to the organisation, and if you are not adding any value, the employers may not want to keep you, and you become vulnerable to layoff.

Lawyers, Doctors, Judges, Health Workers, Police, and Soldiers may not like what they are doing, but they do it. It is their profession; it is their duty. They are professionals, and, in all work, there can be professionals who do their duty even if they don't like it.

Your mind is perceiving dislike and triggering resistance. It is possible to change your mind and create acceptance. Find meaning and purpose in your work; how is your work making a difference in others' lives as well as your own? Understand the bigger picture. Challenge yourself, set a target, establish a process, make use of productivity techniques like Pomodoro, accomplish big goals while working in short intervals, enjoy the flow, and celebrate accomplishments. Take a short vacation if you are experiencing burnout. Make lemonade if you have been handed lemons. It is easier to get an orange if you have a lemon, but if you throw away the lemon before getting an orange, you have nothing.

MALADAPTIVE AND ADAPTIVE STRESS RESPONSE

The maladaptive stress response is an unhealthy, ineffective, and harmful way of dealing with stress. This maladaptive stress response is triggered automatically; it is triggered by our lower brain or animal brain, which is influenced by fear and threat. If you experience any of the maladaptive stress responses being triggered within you, be aware of the negative mental chatter in your mind, be more in control of your mind, and restrain it from leading you into a negative spiral of thoughts. Also, be aware of the negative emotions and feelings; be more in control of your emotions. Be aware of the automatic urge, impulsive behaviour, and automatic, instinctive reactions; remember, these are being triggered by the lower brain, which is making you react like an animal. It will take effort, it may feel uncomfortable, and it is difficult to discipline natural urges, but with willpower and self-control, replace maladaptive responses with adaptive responses.

MALADAPTIVE STRESS RESPONSE SYMPTOMS

- Avoiding problems

- Procrastinating

- Overworking

- Compulsively worrying

- Escapism through alcohol

- Escapism through drugs

- Overeating

- Self-criticism

- Dreading going to work

- Oversleeping

- Depressive feeling

- Social Avoidance

- Rage

- Lashing out at others

- Anxiety

- Rumination, Overthinking

- Denial/Refusal to accept

- Defensiveness

- Resentment

- Helplessness

- Good-For-Nothing Thoughts

- Lack of self-care

- Seeking Sympathy/Self-pity

- Blaming Others

- Self-Doubt

- Fear of Failure

- Impulsive Behaviour.

If you have been experiencing maladaptive behaviour, it is your lower brain or the animal in you which is automatically triggering this behaviour. It is like any animal that feels fear for its life and is in a negative threat mindset. There are urges, cravings, and impulses that are being triggered by the animal within you. But you have to put effort into overcoming this maladaptive response with discipline and self-control. The reason is that maladaptive responses have many adverse consequences on the body and mind. It could lead to chronic stress, which may lead to hypertension, diabetes, heart issues, obesity, digestive problems, headaches, muscle tension, sleep issues, etc. It can contribute to anxiety, depression, and addiction. Think about it: maladaptive behaviour does not solve your problem; you are increasing your problems and also harming your health. Say no to the animal urges; don't let your animal brain control you. Use your intelligence and adaptive response to deal with stress.

ADAPTIVE STRESS RESPONSE

- Problem Solving

- Taking Support

- Taking Self-Care

- Stress-Defusing Techniques

- Breathing Exercise

- Physical Activity

- Being Busy

- Practice Meditation

- Practice Yoga

- Journaling/Writing

- Talking with a friend, sharing with family

- Be good to yourself; be your friend

- Delete or reframe negative thoughts

- Delete/replace negative emotions with positive emotions

- Practice positive self-talk

- Set intentions

- Let go

- Acceptance

- Say no, set boundaries

- Act, adjust, adapt, alter, avoid and adjourn

- Have patience, persist and persevere

- Consider the problem to be a challenge

- This too will pass' attitude

- Limit digital exposure and negative news exposure

- Join a support group

- Accept what it is, it is.

- Whatever will be will be

- Embrace ups and downs, high tides and low tides of life

- Engage in activities that promote laughter

- Sleep, sleep, sleep. Let your mind and body rest.

CHAPTER 4
HOW TO HANDLE NEGATIVE EMOTIONS

"The greatest enemies of success and happiness are negative emotions"

– Brian Tracy

Today MR. Vijay Mallya is a fugitive businessman; there is an effort to extradite him from the UK to India, as he is accused of financial crimes. It is believed that his failed airline, Kingfisher, owes the State-run Bankers around 1.2 billion $ while the assets he had were in excess of 3 billion $. In addition to Kingfisher, he was the chairman of United Spirits, India's largest spirit group, and United Breweries Group, which is also one of the largest breweries groups. He was also chairman of Sanofi India, Bayer Crop Science India, Berger Paints, etc. He could have closed down the loss-making airline, very easily repaid the debts of Kingfisher by selling some of his assets and still left with many billions to live his high-flying life. But he had his king-size ego; he could not fail, so when the debts started mounting, he panicked, but to show that everything was fine, he threw an expensive birthday party, which was bad optics; the press, banks, employees and the government were furious. Mr Mallya feared that he might be arrested for swindling the banks, he got anxious; the animal in him panicked, and he ran away to England, leaving his companies behind; that was a mistake; the enforcing authorities attached all his assets but continued with the effort to extradite him. In India, he became the Public Enemy no 1. His numerous offers to repay the amount he owes to banks on account of Kingfisher Airlines have been rejected because he committed a criminal offence by running away. Why did Mr Mallya run? Why did Mr V.G Siddhartha commit suicide? Why did Siddhant Ganore murder his mother just because she scolded him? The reason could be that the stress became overwhelming, negative emotions like fear and anxiety made them berserk, and they lost control over themselves.

NEGATIVE EMOTIONS

Negative emotions exist in all animals, including humans. All animals experience fear, anxiety, anger, aggression, sadness, etc. These emotions help survival; if fear, anger, aggression, etc, are triggered in the body, it helps that animal fight or flight response. Humans are animals first and humans later; that is, they have an animal brain, and on top of that, the human brain has grown, so if there is a situation which is perceived to be a threat, the instinctive reaction that would be triggered would be an animal response, there would be fear, anxiety, anger, aggression, urge to run away, etc. But humans have the advantage of being self-aware. They can be a higher person if they choose and witness without judging the animal in them getting scared, becoming anxious, getting angry, aggressive, having low mood, procrastinating, having repetitive thoughts; they can witness their increased heart rate and shallow breathing, face getting tense, teeth chattering, headache, discomfort in the stomach, etc. If they detach themselves from the inner animal, they may find it quite amusing how irrational and illogical way the animal in them is reacting; the issue could be some pressure at work, a mismatch of finances, or somebody has said something, but the animal within that human reacts. It may help humans to remind themselves to be humans and control their instincts, unnecessary fears, anxieties, anger, useless aggression, stress, and fight or flight response. Analyse what is bothering them, be Sensible and rational, use their Intelligence (Be SRI), reason and respond like humans.

FEAR

1. Identify what is triggering fear within you. What are you afraid of? When you are emotionally charged, it becomes difficult to think clearly. Write it down. Writing enables a bit more control on yourself as we are disengaged from fear and focus on thinking

and writing. Remember, whatever our brain is getting automatically threatened off is not a threat; they are not going to kill us or injure us. They are problems and challenges in life which are temporary, and there are solutions.

2. Face your fear. What appears to be a monster could be a sheep in a wolf's skin. The animal in you would be afraid. Remember, the animal in you has been programmed to fear the tiger, and it does not want to face the danger. Be gentle with yourself and face the fear gently. It is like a child that does not want to step into the water. Be gentle. Desensitise. Expose it little by little in small, measured steps. Support. Let the child enjoy the water. Its confidence will build up, and it will confidently jump in the next time it faces fear.

3. Talk about your fear with somebody who is not experiencing that fear because that person is not emotionally charged and would be able to analyse the issue calmly and give a better perspective. People who are trained to handle fear, like therapists, counsellors, and mental health professionals, could be of great support. Talking to family and friends helps; there are support groups to join. You can also find support groups online, and if you don't have anybody to talk to, the good old God is always there. You can talk to God about anything, anytime, and you can be sure God will not be judgemental or force its views.

4. The animal in you would have irrational thoughts, catastrophic thoughts which need to be managed. It is not the end of the world; it may be some minor issue like, say, the loss of a job, which may create inconvenience, hardship, discomfort, or embarrassment for a temporary period. If you work out solutions, you may get a new job, or you may find a way of making big money. Challenge your thoughts, reframe them, and calm down the animal in you which is being afraid.

5. Exercise to metabolise the stress hormones and replace negative thoughts with positive ones or memories that make you happy and feel good. Meditation, Mindfulness, Yoga, Relaxation Techniques like Breathing Techniques, Yog Nidra, or just watch a good comedy film that makes you laugh and relax. There are many stress buster exercises that we have included in the chapter ahead; experiment and find out what works best for you.

ANXIETY

The difference between fear and anxiety is that fear is about a situation that is happening now, and anxiety is fear of a situation that may happen in the future. In Eastern spirituality, you are not sure about your next breath; how can you be sure of what will happen in the future? As per the law of karma, the actions that you take today will shape the outcomes and opportunities in the unknown future.

It does not mean don't take care; do take care in providing for an emergency fund, provide for medical insurance, and have a provident fund, but don't be too worried, and don't have anxiety. Oprah Winfrey has rightly said, "Doing your best at this moment puts you in the best place for the next moment." Robert Tew also has rightly said, "Trust yourself, you have survived, you are surviving, you will survive no matter what." A study suggests that ninety-seven percent of the time, what we are anxious about never happens, and if it does happen, people handle it better than they expected.

Having anxious thoughts can be natural as they serve as an alert forewarning and make us cautious. However, anxiety that involves constantly being anxious and persistently having anxious thoughts could lead to Generalised Anxiety Disorder with symptoms such as rapid heartbeat, headache, palpitations, abdominal pain, muscle tension, irritation, trouble concentrating, and difficulty sleeping. It impairs your ability to function normally. Anxiety, which involves fearing that something may happen in the future, a future that is not present for us to act upon, can lead to persistent anxious thoughts. This can affect our mental health. People can suffer from OCD, panic attacks, depression, social isolation, avoidance issues, and health problems, among others.

Worrying about what may happen in the future and whipping yourself for what may happen in the future is being unfair to yourself. What you imagine may happen or may not happen. If it does happen, your resources will determine your action. If it does not happen, you hurt yourself unnecessarily. But by whipping yourself now, you would have hurt your ability to take care of the situation in the future. What is the maximum that can happen? You won't be killed; you won't be hurt. The maximum that can happen, if it happens, is a bit of discomfort and inconvenience, which you can easily handle with a calm mind. Why hurt yourself now for what may happen or may not happen in the future?

The way to handle anxiety would be to write down what is bothering you; many a time, what is bothering you is not as bad as your mind makes it be. There are some views that 97% of the time, what we are anxious about does not happen, or we are able to handle it better than we expected; 3% of the time, if it does happen, work out a contingency plan. If you have a plan of action ready, there is nothing to feel anxious about. Relaxation Techniques like deep breathing, mindfulness, meditation, progressive muscle relaxation, etc., are of great help. Managing thoughts, challenging, deleting, and reframing negative thoughts helps. Exercise helps in metabolising cortisol, the stress hormones released into your body when you get anxious. Talking to someone, taking support. Replacing negative hormones with an activity that triggers happiness and feel-good hormones could also help; feel-good hormones are triggered by feel-good activities like laughing, playing, dancing, singing, drawing, meeting friends, sharing, having gratitude, watching comedy shows, enjoying great games, helping others, etc. Mark Twain often laced humour with profound wisdom. Some of his quotes on anxiety were, "Worrying is like paying a debt you don't owe" and "I had a lot of worries in my life, most of which never happened." Dalai Lama famously said, "If a situation is such that you can do something about it, then there is no need to worry. If the situation is such that you cannot do something about it, then there is no help in worrying." Throw to the universe what is bothering you, and you cannot do anything about it; the universe will always find what is good for you" By allowing yourself to get anxious, you achieve nothing but lose many things.

This is a story about a friend who was constantly worried about his son. The son had dropped out of college and spent his time locked up, playing computer games. The son was obsessed with computer games and created his own games, but the son's passion was not understood by his father, who was pushing the son to follow what he felt would be good for him. There was a lot of tension in that house: constant arguments, hostility, showdowns, and anger. The father suffered from a heart condition and other stress-related diseases. He died because of a heart attack. During the mourning period, his son received an acceptance for a proof of concept that he had submitted to one of the world's largest gaming companies based in Japan. He received funding for developing the concept for a computer game, and the investment that he got was more money than wilder than the wildest the family could ever think of. Today, he has set up a company in a small district located in Southern India, making computer games for companies based in Japan and America. Last year, his turnover was in excess of 800 crores (100 million). His father would have been very proud of his son today, but unfortunately, his father died because of the pressure that he had put on his heart because his son had not followed his dream for him. The dreams and destinies of others are not in our control; stressing our bodies for something that is not in our control is unfair to our bodies. Sometimes, being of support to somebody helping them find their dream helps instead of telling them what to do, which they may not want to do.

NEGATIVE THOUGHT PATTERNS

In the original scheme of things of nature, humans came in the category of prey animals. Negative thinking helps prey survive; humans would have a bias towards negative thinking. But today, the challenges have changed. There are hardly any threats to survival but a requirement to thrive in the human ecosystem, which requires positive thinking and a positive attitude. However, negative thinking is a bad habit in us, and we need to change our habits.

There can be negative consequences due to negative thought patterns. It can trigger negative emotions like anxiety and depression, create health issues, impair brain function and decision-making ability, and take us on a downward spiral. Some negative thought patterns include Personalisation, which is taking blame for events outside your control; Magnification, which is over-exaggerating implications and imagining a worst-case scenario; Catastrophising, which involves making a catastrophe out of normal adverse events or situations and believing that the world will end; Negative Filtering, where some people only focus on negative things, expecting sympathy, being pessimists who are always in a depressed mood and have poor self-esteem; Jumping to conclusions, making unwarranted assumptions, and discounting the positives. These are called cognitive distortions. Negative thought patterns could be due to strong negative influences or a negativity bias and often become self-fulfilling prophecies. How to reduce negative thought patterns.

- Identify Negative Thoughts: Be more mindful of your thoughts. Are you deprecating yourself, blaming yourself, catastrophising, exaggerating, expecting only negatives to happen, discounting the positives in life, feeling fear, anxiety, worries, etc.?

- Challenge Negative Thoughts: Negative thoughts are not harmless. Your primal brain perceives negative thoughts as a threat and could trigger a stress response, disturbing the balance in your body. You don't need be a tragedy king or queen, playing the victim card and also it would be unfair to blame yourself. Be SRI sensible, be rational, be intelligent; The animal in you may have irrational thoughts. The human in you needs to control those thoughts.

- Reframe thoughts: Whether the glass is half full or half empty depends on how you view it. Feeling bad or good is influenced by how you perceive or interpret a situation. Due to our animal legacy, we tend to perceive most situations negatively because of a negative bias. However, in our endeavour to be more human, reframing our thoughts and shifting towards positivity would be beneficial.

- Mindfulness: being mindful about thoughts helps reduce negative thoughts, helps stay present, and reduces obsessive-compulsive thoughts, that is, ruminations, having the same negative thoughts again and again.

- Journal: Many times, it becomes difficult to have clarity about our thoughts when thoughts are triggering. Neurons are firing in our brains; there may be no cohesion, and there could be a lot of confusion. The emotions triggered by thoughts create imbalance. It is difficult to think rationally. Writing it down or journaling has an advantage; your brain gets more focused, and your eyes get engaged in writing, so they stop wandering, stopping the triggering of random thoughts. You are physically engaged because your hands are occupied. This compels you to be more logical and sensible, have more clarity, and reduce your negative thought pattern.

- CBT: Cognitive Behavioural Therapy is a type of talk therapy that can help identify and challenge negative thoughts and behaviours. It can help people learn to think more positively and realistically and replace negative beliefs. CBT is based on the concept that negative thinking is a bad habit that can be changed. CBT helps people notice their negative thought patterns and reframe them to change the perspective. Automatic negative thoughts affect mood, create emotional difficulties, and can lead to anxiety and depression. CBT helps to reframe negative thoughts and look at issues more realistically.

STRESSFUL LIFE EVENTS

Stressful life events that can cause depression include grief due to the loss of a loved one, breakup in a relationship, conflicts, divorce, job loss, financial problems, health issues, a toxic work environment, job insecurity, inability to cope with work, major life changes, negative self-perception, loneliness, lack of social support, emotional, physical, and sexual abuse and other non-acceptable thoughts or behaviour.

As mentioned earlier, the strategy to cope with a stressful life can include sharing, talking to someone, taking professional help, joining a support group, mindfulness, meditation, yoga, exercise to reduce the stress hormone cortisol, having a hobby, and doing what you like to do. Avoidance or escapism tactics like taking drugs and alcohol abuse can badly misfire. Historically, many people have been able to cope with stressful life events by being spiritual. They believe that challenges in life are there to test or to learn, or to evolve us as better versions of ourselves, the test of being human. They adopt the attitude that no matter what life throws at them, they will not be distracted from their higher purpose of life, which is to be human. They will not be animals; they will not get stressed; they will not fight or run. They will reason and respond like humans; they will live life, be happy, be useful, and be and stay responsible. There would be stressful life events, but stress is your response to these events; you can choose not to get stressed.

ANGER

Anger, personalised thought with resistance, is also a natural emotion that is triggered in response to a perceived threat. Anger is helpful for fighting or running; if the animal is angry, then it can more aggressively defend itself. Anger and aggression are some of the emotions that enhance fight or flight, and that is the stress response. Anger is influenced by how a person interprets or thinks about a situation. If a person perceives or interprets a situation to be a threat to life, then that person could get angry and could get stressed. Because the situation is processed automatically, perceiving or interpretation is done automatically, and anger and stress are triggered automatically.

Anger has its advantages as it expresses disapproval and sets boundaries. It could be a protective mechanism as it would motivate action when there is injustice or bad unacceptable behaviour, but it is important to have control over oneself. This control could determine when, with whom, and how much to get angry because anger, if not controlled, can lead to negative consequences.

Anger, like stress, can lead to health issues such as high blood pressure, heart disease, stomach ailments, and pressure on the brain. It can contribute to anxiety, depression, and other mental health issues. It can damage relationships with family, friends, and colleagues, thus adding to your problems. Anger can make a person make impulsive, irrational decisions that may have negative consequences. Anger can make a person aggressive, leading to violence, which can have its own repercussions. Anger could lead to conflicts with colleagues and seniors that may create problems at the workplace and could also result in job loss.

The way to handle anger is to recognise the trigger, be aware of the symptoms, and be prepared with a strategy or toolkit not to get angry. There are techniques to distract oneself, change thoughts, use humour, communicate that you are getting angry, take time out, etc. A cool-down technique, wherein you deeply breathe out through your mouth and then deeply breathe in through your nose, is also helpful. Deep breathing exercises, meditation, mindfulness, and yoga are useful for anger issues. Learn to say "NO," Avoid people or situations causing anger, seek support, and talk to people or professionals trained to handle anger issues. Maintaining a journal where you can express your feelings and emotions is helpful. Physical exercise is important as it metabolises stress hormones. You can make fundamental changes to the way you respond by reframing or having a different perspective of what you perceive as a threat. Do maintain a stress book, make a note of your reactions, emotions, and feelings, and identify the underlying reason. Anger, fear, anxiety, stress, depression, etc., are our animal instincts, natural responses to threats, but the threats for which these natural responses were made have changed. Therefore, these natural responses are now inappropriate. Change your response, be 'SRI', be human, be sensible, be rational, and use your intelligence and reason. If you are prepared with a response, there could be less automatic, natural response, less anger, fear, anxiety, stress, and depression.

MISTAKES

Although a mistake may not be an emotion, making a mistake triggers all kinds of emotions. Making a mistake can be frustrating and demotivating, but making a mistake is a natural part of the learning process. People become experts in their field by learning from their mistakes. If you make a mistake, reflect on what went wrong and why. When you make a mistake, it is etched in your memory, and the likelihood of repeating the same mistake is reduced. The more mistakes you make, the more you learn and the more expertise you gain. Instead of beating yourself up, look at it as an opportunity to grow. Everybody makes mistakes; it is how mistakes are handled that matters. If you are feeling overwhelmed, break the task into smaller, more manageable tasks. If your mind is procrastinating, gradually lead your mind with limited exposure and gently guide it towards accepting the mistake and moving forward with life. Mindfulness, meditation, positive self-talk, sharing, talking with someone who understands, thought-stopping, and getting busy with work and life are helpful in overcoming the stress of having made a mistake.

UNCERTAINTY AND INSECURITY

Again, uncertainty and insecurity may not be emotions, but they trigger negative emotions and stress. While I was writing this book, there were many news reports about layoffs in the tech-based industry and the redundancy struggles of senior people in that industry after the age of forty. Their responsibilities have increased, but so have the insecurity and uncertainty. While I don't claim to have any answers to industry-specific queries about what they should do, I do suggest, as far as practicable, not to get stressed. Why do I say "as far as practicable?" Because I have gone through stress while preaching not to get stressed. In reality, it is very difficult for a simple reason: there are going to be many demands and requirements. The insecurity of not getting a paycheck could be very threatening. Our radar is going to pick up the negative signals. There are going to be negative thoughts, and negative thoughts could trigger fear, anxiety, anger, and stress. There could be low mood and depressive feelings. This is a natural response and happens automatically, but from my experience, I would say this natural automatic response is not helpful; it makes you fearful and anxious, there are repetitive thoughts, and physical discomforts like headache, tension, and pounding head make it difficult to reason, stress makes you tunnel-visioned, and it becomes difficult to consider other factors, alternate solution. But if you refuse to allow yourself to get automatically stressed, have self-control and use your intellect, you may find the solutions to be simpler than what your mind makes you believe. Stress does not help but creates many disadvantages. The problems or challenges you face in life are temporary; they go away, but the problems that you can create in your body by getting stressed, like heart issues, blood pressure issues, diabetes, stomach issues, etc, can impact the quality of life in the long term. The situations in life are not in our control; what is the maximum that can happen? There could be temporary discomfort; by using your intelligence, you may find solutions to most of the situations, or you may be able to adjust or adapt. It makes sense to accept the situation, avoid resistance, and avoid getting stressed.

THE ANIMAL AND THE HUMAN WITHIN

The concept of the "lower brain" and "upper brain" often refers to the interplay between primitive and advanced brain functions that govern human behaviour. These concepts are sometimes explained using evolutionary neuroscience, distinguishing between reactive and rational aspects of human psychology.

Lower Brain: The Animal Within Human

The lower brain includes regions like the amygdala, brainstem and limbic system. These areas are responsible for primal instincts, survival mechanisms, and emotional reactivity. The characteristics of the lower or animal brain include:

Fear and Anxiety: Immediate responses to perceived threats (fight or flight)

Anger: Protective aggression triggered by challenges or danger.

Depression: A response to prolonged stress, often tied to feelings of helplessness.

Reactivity and Stress: Quick, automatic responses without thinking.

This "animal brain" ensures survival by responding to danger and challenges. For ancient human, the animal brain is helpful for quick response against threat and even for modern human it is of big help, when somebody is physically attacking you or quick responses are required to avoid accidents.

The issue is that nature has made this quick response part of our automatic nervous system, so if our brain perceives a threat, our automatic nervous system triggers stress, and our brain also works automatically; the eyes, ears, nose, touch, feelings, memory are sending automatic information, our brain without applying its mind, is automatically interpreting and it is automatically triggering fight or flight response. This puts the modern human in an awkward situation; they may react like animals in situations which they don't like, like missing a train, workers not reporting for work, being asked to do overtime or reading news that some bat has fallen sick in China. They start beating themselves; think about it: what are we doing to ourselves when we get stressed? We increase our heartbeat, increase blood pressure, get angry, upset, and lose sleep, but how is that going to help us address our issues? It does not. Nature did not anticipate that a cousin of the chimpanzee would use their brain and start solving their problem and become human, so till nature changes its design, humans should use their intelligence and control their reactions; they should observe the antics of the animal within, how it gets fear, anger, anxious, worry, upset, frustrated, keeps on having negative thoughts, humans have to keep on reminding themselves to be human.

The Upper Brain: The Human Within Human

The upper brain refers to the prefrontal cortex and other higher-order brain areas that allow for advanced reasoning and self-regulation. The characteristics of the upper brain include:

Sensible and Rational Thinking: Problem-solving and understanding consequences.

Intelligence and Reasoning: Logical decision-making based on evidence.

Self-Control: Overriding impulsive emotions to act thoughtfully.

Human Spirit: Compassion, creativity and pursuit of meaning and values.

The upper brain allows humans to transcend primal instincts, fostering growth and development, harmony and fulfilment.

Challenge Mentality: Meeting of Human Intelligence with Animal Spirit

The challenge mentality integrates the lower brains drive and upper brain's intelligence. It uses the energy and instinct of the "animal within" (competitiveness, courage, perseverance etc) in a directed and constructive way.

Harnessing Instincts: Utilising fear or aggression as motivation rather than letting them dominate.

Strategic Thinking: Combining emotional drive with rational planning.

Resilience: Facing challenges head-on with determination instead of avoiding them.

Creativity: Transforming reactive energy into productive outcomes.

This approach represents a balanced state where the primal instincts fuel effort, but the upper brain ensures this effort aligns with logic, rational thinking, long-term goals and values. To summarise. The lower Brain is reactive, emotional, and survival-oriented (animal nature). The upper Brain is rational, self-regulated, and oriented (human nature). Challenge Mentality synergises the use of both, leveraging primal instincts through intelligence for constructive action. Developing awareness of these dynamics can help individuals overcome stress, achieve personal growth, and lead more fulfilling lives by channelling raw emotions into purposeful, rational actions.

CHAPTER 5
HOW MR. AMITABH BACHCHAN REDUCED STRESS

"Bad luck either destroys or makes you discover the strength in you."

– Bachchan

STORY OF MR AMITABH BACHCHAN

If we understand how Mr. Amitabh Bachchan, one of the most popular stars of the Indian film industry, reduced his stress, we may be able to figure out some techniques to deal with modern-day challenges. The story is that Amitabh Bachchan was nearly bankrupt in 2000. Amitabh Bachchan Corporation Ltd., the company that he had promoted to transform the entertainment industry, had failed. The company had borrowed heavily, and Mr Bachchan had given a personal guarantee for the loan that was taken by his company. The company had hardly any assets, so the creditors attached Mr. Bachchan's personal assets to recover the loans. **Mr.** Bachchan was nearly 58 years of age when he got into trouble. At an age where most people want to retire and look forward to a peaceful, settled life, **Mr.** Bachchan faced an unsettled future. He had no bank balance, his property was attached, and it was humiliating to see an attachment notice on the wall of Pratiksha, the place where he stayed. It was humiliating to face the creditors. He was not getting any work because many of his recent films had flopped, and many producers were unhappy with him when his company entered the film production business. However, the way **Mr.** Bachchan dealt with his challenges holds many lessons in dealing with modern-day challenges. The mindset that seems to have helped **Mr.** Bachchan also seems to have helped most of the famous personalities who overcame difficult challenges. Let us see how Mr Bachchan dealt with his challenges.

MR BACHCHAN WAS BEING HUMAN

Mr Bachchan was being human because he controlled his emotions; he controlled stress that was naturally getting triggered in him. He was rational and sensible; he knew that getting angry, upset, or aggressive is not going to help him. What may help him is to be calm and relaxed and use his intellect to analyse the problem he was in, work out various solutions, take action, and arrive at a solution that works. Mr Bachchan also had patience. He dealt with bureaucrats calmly. Despite rejections by Film producers, he calmly approached them. When creditors were hounding him, he called them up with a request not to put pressure on him. He was working on solutions to pay them off. He refused to blame anybody and refused to react when people employed by him who had made mistakes made statements like he was not fit to be a businessman. He refused to get emotional or get stressed by the problem he was facing. He was being human, and that helped him manage his challenge.

MR BACHCHAN HAD A CHALLENGE MINDSET

Mr. Bachchan, in that situation where he was nearly bankrupt, had a challenge mindset. He refused to get anxious, be afraid, or feel helpless. He was not agitated, aggressive, or angry. He knew the situation was difficult but not something that was overwhelming. He never got distracted by creditors who used to land up at his residence and abuse the family. He did not get distracted by the many legal notices and summons. He refused to get frustrated for not getting acting work. He assessed his marketable skills; in addition to acting, he could be a great host. He had a great voice which he could use for voice-overs. He had a great personality that portrayed trust and dignity, which could be leveraged for Brand Campaigns. His confidence, excitement, and enthusiasm were visible when he did the television show "Kaun Banega Crorepati" . He was in control and focused on finding ways and means to earn money, pay off his debts, and earn a living.

MR BACCHAN HAD A POSITIVE ATTITUDE

Mr Bachchan had a positive attitude. He chose to see and respond to negative situations with positive attitude. He refused to entertain fear, anxiety, anger, upset, depression etc. He began to explore solutions, had faith, hope, optimism and courage. Believed that problems are temporary and everything will turn out better. He refused to get stressed, filled his day with activity, kept himself busy, refused to get frustrated by rejections and kept on working at different options to work out solutions.

MR BACHCHAN ACCEPTED THE SITUATION

To understand acceptance and non-acceptance of the situation, I will share story of another mega star of Indian film industry who was contemporary of Mr Bachchan. This gentleman was bigger success, time changed but this person refused to change, it was stupid to see an older man playing a role of college student, romancing actress, less than half his age. The industry had got professionalised and nobody had time or inclination to put up with tantrums and famously coming late to the film sets dramas. His films flopped, he refused to accept the situation, he refused to change, he started drinking, putting on more weight, abused his wife and children, got lonely, he was not getting any film role and was too proud to work on televisions, suffered illness alone, he died alone and his body was found two days after he had passed away. Huge crowd was there in his funeral but nobody had been there, when he was in trouble.

Mr Bachchan accepted the situation, kept away from alcohol, drugs or any form of escapism, he connected with his friend and family, regularly had talk with them, inspite of being abandoned by some of the producers, always maintained respect, conducted self in humility and dignity, he is known to be punctual for work and never throws any tantrums or has any starry air about self. When film as hero was not being offered, he had no qualms of working as character actor, he had no qualms of being television host or being voice over artist.

MR BACHCHAN ADJUSTED, ADAPTED, AND ALTERED

The lesson that we can learn from the way Mr Bachchan dealt with his challenges is also that of adjustment. As the family faced financial challenges, Mr Bachchan adjusted his lifestyle to be within his means. His son Abhishek Bachchan was studying at Boston University in America. Senior Mr Bachchan informed his son that the family's current finances were not able to support his foreign education. Mr Abhishek Bachchan discontinued his studies in America, came back to India, started getting coached in dialogue delivery in Hindi, and enhanced his acting skills. Junior Mr Bachchan also started to look for acting assignments to supplement family income. Senior Mr Bachchan also reduced his staff and overhead expenses. Mr Bachchan adjusted himself to television. He took up the assignment of being the background narrator for the film "Lagaan" and accepted a supporting role in his comeback movie, "Mohabbatein," where the main hero was Shahrukh Khan. He started accepting more mature roles and reinvented himself from an angry young man to a quirky old man. Mr Bachchan adjusted, adapted, and altered himself to the situation. According to Darwin's *Origin of Species*, it is not the intellect or the strongest that survives; the species that survives is the one that is best able to adjust and adapt to the changing environment in which it finds itself.

MR BACHCHAN AVOIDED

Mr Bachchan's challenges also teach us what to avoid. He avoided blaming anyone. He avoided reacting to nasty comments and backbiting. He avoided litigating and focused on finding a solution to his problem. He avoided getting angry, upset, irritated, or frustrated about his problem. He avoided compounding his problem and getting into double trouble, that is, getting irritated and angry and creating friction with his family and friends because of the problem he was facing. He avoided alcohol, he avoided drugs, he avoided cigarettes, he avoided brooding about his problem or wallowing in self-pity. He avoided overthinking and losing sleep and just focused on working towards a solution to his problem. He avoided getting stressed.

MR BACHCHAN TOOK CHARGE

In the initial stage, there was a lot of speculation about the amount of money ABCL owed. Mr Bachchan, instead of delegating, took personal charge of his situation. He held meetings with his bankers, creditors, tax consultants, and lawyers, seeking advice from specialised consultants. He realised that the actual amount owed was much less than what was being speculated. When the creditors were assured that he wanted to repay the debt of the Company from his personal funds, they empathised with him and worked out terms that would make it easy for him to repay. There are unconfirmed reports that Mr Bachchan opted for a One-Time Settlement, and the actual amount that he had to pay was far less than what was being reported. Mr Bachchan made an effort to understand the problem that he was in, which is not easy because many times, when you are in a difficult situation, there could be an emotional hijack. It becomes difficult to think straight; the brain could get clouded, and anger and irritation create a deterrent to getting the required calmness to understand the actual problem and work out a solution. There could be automatic low mood, not feeling like it, a feeling of procrastination where you would want to avoid facing the problem, and a depressive feeling may also get triggered in the body.

Mr Bachchan could have been aware of the emotions that were triggered by the nervous animal within him, but he could have controlled them with emotional control techniques. Objectively, he could analyse his situation and work out solutions for his problem. Charles Kettering, the head of research at General Motors, had famously said, *"Understanding the problem is half the solution."* The ability to exert control over our emotions helps us understand the problem. Emotions and stress are triggered by the nervous animal in us, which has fear, gets angry and upset, triggers stress in our body, and activates our body to respond like an animal. The fact is that the modern problems that we are facing are just problems and challenges in life. They are not a threat to our existence. They are not life and death situations; there are solutions to all problems in life if we deal with them like humans, that is, *"Be rational, reason and resolve response"* instead of reacting like an animal, that is, *"Getting emotional getting stressed fight or flight response."*

MR BACHCHAN TOOK CARE OF SELF

One thing that has been observed about most of the celebrities who came out of difficult situations is that they took care of themselves. That is, they did not let the negative situation or the negative mood that was triggered by the negative situation overpower them and make them neglect to take care of themselves. A negative situation for them was one aspect of life that they were temporarily facing, but that was not life itself. Mr Bachchan did yoga, exercised, and meditated. He believed in a higher power and was known to pray. He made a schedule and engaged himself by focusing outside and doing productive work. There is research that suggests that humans are more stressed and depressed because they spend more time lost in thoughts, ruminating, etc. Our mind is inclined towards being negative; there is constant chatter in the mind. If you are facing a negative situation, there could be repetitive thoughts reminding you about the negative situation. There is a reason for this; our mind is triggering those thoughts because it wants to alert you, make you cautious, and get you prepared for fight or flight. But as explained earlier, these are obsolete responses because the challenges that we are facing are different, requiring us to be calmer and more relaxed to be more creative and innovative. Mr Bachchan made it a point to share; he maintained a diary where he would put down his thoughts. He made it a point to discuss this with his family. His son became his great friend in the trying circumstances. He did not smoke, did not have alcohol, did not consume drugs, and slept early. He is known to watch movies and learn more about his craft. These are all great learnings. There could be challenges in life; they may not be in your control, but you do have control over your response. Stress can create an imbalance in our body; We add to the imbalance by not taking care of ourselves.

CHAPTER 6
UNIQUE CONCEPTS TO REDUCE STRESS

In today's fast-paced world, stress has become a ubiquitous companion in our lives. We often perceive stress as an unavoidable byproduct of modern challenges - work pressures, personal responsibilities, societal expectations and unforeseen setbacks. The real issue is not stress but our reactions to life's problems and challenges. Stress, at its core, is a reflection of how we interpret, process and respond to our circumstances; while external factors may trigger it, the key to managing stress lies within us. Addressing stress without tackling the root cause often results in temporary relief. Short-term remedies, distractions, escapism, etc, may alleviate symptoms but fail to provide long-term resilience. What truly makes a difference is adopting a holistic approach that focuses on solving problems and developing strategies to reduce stress at its core.

This chapter introduces nine **unique** and **transformative concepts** that empower you to rethink and reshape your relationship with stress. Each concept offers practical wisdom, inspired by diverse philosophies, cultures and mindsets, it is designed to equip you with the tools to lead a more balanced and fulfilling life. These approaches challenge conventional stress management techniques, offering innovative perspectives that prioritise personal growth, acceptance and proactive problem solving.

The Unique Concepts are, Being Stoic, Stress Dairy, Avoid Triple Trouble, Shouganai and Ukeireru, Que Sera, Sera, Wabi - Sabi, living in Tao, Paradigm Shift and Fix the Roof.

BEING STOIC

Stoic philosophy offers a powerful approach to reducing stress by altering how we perceive and respond to challenging situations. Stress is a defensive mechanism. It is an evolutionary response designed to protect us from immediate threats. This "fight or flight response is triggered when our mind perceives a situation as threatening or negative. However, in modern life, most of the stressors are not life-threatening but are perceived as such because of our emotional and cognitive reactions. Stress does not stem directly from the situation but from how we interpret and emotionally respond to it. Two people can face the same situation but experience different levels of stress based on their perception and thought patterns.

Stoicism teaches us to focus on what we can control and accept what we cannot. If we don't label a situation as "bad" or "negative," our defence system won't perceive it as a threat. Without this trigger, the stress response is minimised. For instance, viewing a job loss as an opportunity for growth rather than a failure reduces stress significantly. There is a difference between Animal and Human Responses. Animals react instinctively to challenges - fear, aggression, or escape dominate their behaviour. Humans, however, have the capacity for rationality, self-awareness, and emotional regulation. Instead of reacting impulsively, we can pause, assess and respond thoughtfully.

To embody Stoicism in daily life, consider these steps:

Acceptance: Recognise that some events are beyond your control. Resistance to those realities only amplifies stress. Acceptance doesn't mean giving up. It means conserving energy for areas where you can make a difference.

Adjust, Adapt, Alter: Flexibility is key. Adjust your mindset, adapt to new realities, or alter your plans to align with the situation. This approach keeps you proactive rather than reactive.

Avoid or Adjourn: Sometimes, the best course of action is to step back or delay responding until emotions have subsided. A calm mind can often find solutions that a stressed mind cannot.

Take Action When Possible: Stress often arises from feeling powerless. Taking small, deliberate actions to address challenges gives you a sense of control, reducing the helplessness that fuels stress.

Viewing Life as a Test of Humanity

Stoicism encourages seeing every challenge as an opportunity to practice virtues such as patience, courage, wisdom and resilience. This approach would help reframe situations.

Financial Problems or Job Loss: Instead of despair, see these as tests of your ability to be resourceful and resilient. What can you learn? What new paths can you explore?

Professional Challenges: View work pressure or setbacks as opportunities to grow stronger and more skilled. Focus on what you can improve rather than lamenting what went wrong.

Uncertainty and Insecurity: There is going to be uncertainty and insecurity in life. Rather than fearing the unknown, cultivate trust in your ability to adapt to whatever comes.

Sensible Responses: Analyse **the** situation calmly. Ask yourself, "Is this within my control? If not, how can I adjust my mindset?

Rational Thinking: Focus on facts rather than assumptions or fears. For example, instead of thinking, "I'll never recover from this," reframe it as, "This is a setback, but I have the strength to rebuild.

Intelligent Actions: Make decisions based on long-term outcomes rather than short-term emotions.

By accepting and responding thoughtfully to challenges, you create a sense of calm and control. Each time you overcome a challenge with grace, you build mental and emotional strength. Adopting a stoic approach transforms adversity into an opportunity to live with purpose, dignity and wisdom. In essence, being stoic doesn't mean suppressing emotions or becoming indifferent. It means mastering your mind to align your responses with your higher self, turning every challenge into a stepping stone for personal growth.

STRESS DIARY

A stress diary is a simple yet effective tool to reduce or manage stress. It helps identify stress triggers and patterns in daily life. A stress diary is a log where you record stressful events, your emotions, and physical responses to them. The principle of Stress Diary is that there is something about the event that is bothering you or you are feeling threatened about something, and that is triggering a fight-or-flight response from your body; there are negative emotions like fear, anxiety, anger, sadness, irritation, etc. There could be physical responses like shallow breathing, heart rate, tension, headache, discomfort, etc. The idea is to figure out what is bothering you and the underlying reason for stress, and instead of a fifth or flight response, getting stressed, replace that with reason and respond, that is, work out a response that is sensible, rational and intelligent.

The stress diary is used in the first column, "Record the Date and Time." In the second column, "Describe the Event." In the third column, "Note the emotional and physical response," and in the fourth column," Think about a response that would have been more sensible, rational and intelligent," For example, in the first column, 5th December, 9.15 am, Second Column, "Got stuck in Traffic." Third Column: "Got upset, angry, felt my blood pressure increasing. "Fourth Column "Plan to leave at 8.30 am to avoid Traffic. Stress is an unhelpful response, but it is triggered instinctively. In modern times, the same event or situation may repeat, but if you have already worked out a response that is sensible, rational, and intelligent, you would be better prepared not to respond with stress. There may not be a solution for every event or solution, but a stress control response could also be a good response. For example, you have missed a work deadline, and your response was that you felt anxious, your heart was racing, and your head was pounding. You can replace that with sensible responses, missed work deadlines, response and control stress with the "cool-down technique."

AVOID TRIPLE TROUBLE

The concept "Avoid Triple Trouble" emphasises the importance of handling challenges rationally to prevent problems from escalating. It encourages people to avoid compounding an initial issue by adding emotional, physical, and relational stress to it. Here's a breakdown:

First Trouble - The Problem Itself

When faced with a challenge, say financial issue, work issue, relationship or any other issue, the primary focus should be on understanding and addressing the problem rationally.

Second Trouble - Emotional and Physical Reactions

Allowing anxiety, anger, or emotional distress to take over not only distracts you from solving the issue but also impacts your health. Stress can lead to elevated blood pressure, stomach acid, and other physical problems, effectively doubling your trouble.

Third Trouble - Social Conflict

Emotional reactions like anger or frustration can strain relationship with family, friends, or colleagues. This leads to arguments, hostility, and additional stress, further compounding the problem.

By managing emotions, controlling stress responses, and focusing on finding solutions, you avoid multiplying your troubles. Approaching challenges with a calm and rational mindset not only preserves your health and relationship but also helps resolve the issues more effectively. The essence of "Avoid Triple Trouble" lies in reducing stress by addressing problems directly rather than letting them spiral into larger challenges.

SHOUGANAI and UKEIRERU

The concepts of Shouganai and Ukeireru are deeply rooted in Japanese philosophy and can be powerful tools for stress reduction. They emphasise the importance of acceptance and mental adaptability in managing life's challenges.

"Shouganai" means 'It cannot be helped or 'It is what it is." Shouganai encourages letting go of things beyond your control instead of resisting the circumstances that cannot be changed. It suggests acknowledging their inevitability. This mindset helps reduce stress by preventing unnessacary emotional turmoil over situations you can't influence.

For example, if there is setback or failure, instead of complaining or stressing over it. Shouganai reminds you to adapt and move forward without wasting energy on frustration.

"Ukeireru "means 'To accept' or 'Acceptance.' Ukeireru teaches acceptance of life's complexities-yourself, others, circumstances around you. This principle encourages a compassionate and non-judgemental approach to life, fostering peace and emotional resilience. For example: When faced with personal flaws or the imperfections of others. Ukeireru inspires you to embrace these realities with understanding rather than resistance.

Adopting the philosophy of Shouganai and Ukeireru can help reduce stress by: -

- **Letting Go of Control:** Stress often stems from trying to control the uncontrollable. By practising Shouganai, you can focus on what is within your influence and let go of what is not

- **Reducing Emotional Turmoil:** Resisting reality leads to frustration and imbalance. Ukeireru promotes emotional harmony by teaching acceptance of both the good and the bad.

- **Fostering Inner Peace:** Accepting life's unpredictability reduces anxiety and fosters a sense of calm. Instead of being overwhelmed by external factors, these principles encourage one to approach challenges with reason and composure.

- **Improving Relationship:** Accepting people as they are (Ukeireru) helps build stronger, more harmonious relationships, reducing interpersonal stress.

The Japanese culture's emphasis on these principles contributes to their collective resilience, calm demeanour, and, potentially, their long life expectancy. By not fixating on external disturbances or internal imperfections, they maintain a balanced life that promotes mental and physical health. Incorporating Shouganai and Ukeireru into daily life can empower one to face stress with grace and build a mindset centred on peace, acceptance and reason.

"QUE SERA, SERA"

The phrase "Que Sera, Sera" embodies a philosophy of acceptance and trust in the unpredictability of life. When applied to reducing anxiety, it offers a powerful perspective: rather than becoming consumed by fears of what might happen in the future, we accept that the future is unknowable and trust in our ability to handle whatever comes our way. Anxiety often stems from the fear of the unknown and anticipation of negative outcomes. The mind creates imagined scenarios as if they are real threats. This triggers a physiological stress response, flooding the body with stress hormones like cortisol and adrenaline. This response was evolutionarily designed to help us escape predators, but it is often unnecessary in modern situations. As a result, sleep is disrupted. Rational thinking is impaired, and emotional and physical well-being is compromised.

When we embrace the idea of Que Sera, Sera. "Whatever will be, will be:

- **Release Control:** Recognise that not everything is within our control, and that's okay. This reduces the need to anticipate every possible outcome.

- **Trust Your Abilities:** Even if challenges arise, trust in your intellect, problem-solving skills, and resilience to navigate through them.

- **Focus on the Present:** Anxiety pulls one to the future, which may just be one's imagination. Adopting a "Que Sera, Sera" attitude grounds one in the present, enabling one to respond thoughtfully rather than react impulsively.

The benefit of this attitude is that one lets go of excessive worry. Stress hormones in the body are decreased. The fight-or-flight response, which is stress, is minimised. Cognitive clarity improves, enabling better decision-making. Emotional well-being is preserved, leading to better mood and relationships. Physical health issues linked to stress, such as high blood pressure and digestive problems, are mitigated. What is the worst that can happen? Most setbacks result in temporary inconveniences rather than catastrophic outcomes. Recognising this can transform fear into manageable challenges. Approaching life with the attitude of "Que Sera, Sera" makes one better prepared mentally, emotionally and physically to face whatever comes. Live in the present, trust the ability to adapt, release unnecessary worry, and foster a peaceful, resilient mindset. Que Sera, Sera.

WABI-SABI IS A JAPANESE PHILOSOPHY THAT CELEBRATES IMPERFECTION

Wabi-Sabi celebrates the beauty of imperfection and impermanence in life. It teaches us to find grace in flaws and appreciate life's natural state. By adopting this perspective, we can see that imperfection is not something to be feared but something to be embraced. Perfection is a double-edged sword. While the pursuit of excellence can inspire us to achieve great things, the constant demand for perfection often traps us in an endless cycle of stress, self-doubt and frustration. At its core, perfectionism stems from the belief that anything less than perfect is a failure, but this mindset comes with a heavy price, stress, loss of peace of mind, bitterness and a tag of incompetence because the project does not meet timelines so critical for modern-day working. Perfection is not the same as striving for excellence. While striving for excellence encourages growth, creativity and effort, perfectionism is rooted in fear of making mistakes, fear of judgement, and fear of not being good enough. This fear creates a relentless pressure that often leads to:

Chronic Stress: The constant pursuit of perfection creates an unrealistic standard that is nearly impossible to achieve. This leads to perpetual stress as we push ourselves to meet unattainable expectations.

Procrastination: Paradoxically, perfectionists often delay tasks because the fear of not achieving perfection can be paralysing. This procrastination leads to more stress and less productivity.

Burnout: The unrelenting effort to be perfect leads to overthinking, drains energy, frustration, stress, leaving no time for rest and recovery. Overtime, this can lead to mental and physical exhaustion.

Reduced Creativity and Growth: When perfection becomes the goal, the focus shifts from learning and exploring to avoiding mistakes. This stifles creativity and hinders personal and professional growth leading to stress and disappointment, lack of societal recognition.

Reducing perfectionism is not about lowering standards or settling for mediocrity; it's about setting realistic goals and valuing progress over perfection. Redefine success; start by questioning your definition of success. Is success about achieving flawless results, or is it about growth, learning and effort? By focusing on progress rather than perfection, you can celebrate small wins and acknowledge your efforts, even if the outcome isn't perfect. Embrace mistakes. Mistakes are not failures; they are opportunities to learn and grow. Accepting that errors are a natural part of life can help you approach challenges with a healthier mindset. Instead of fearing mistakes, view them as valuable feedback. Focus on the bigger picture. Ask yourself if this matter will be a year or five years from now. What matters is time. We all have limited time available to us, and time is irreplaceable. Often, the things we obsess over lose their importance with time. Shifting your focus to the bigger picture helps put perfectionism into perspective and reduces unnecessary stress. Your health and happiness are more important than any perfect outcome. Stressing oneself and others to attain perfection is not helpful.

LIVING IN TAO

"Living in Tao" is a concept that is rooted in Taoism, an ancient Chinese philosophy often called "The Way." Tao's emphasis is living in harmony with the natural order of the universe and the flow of life.

Acceptance of Natural Flow: Instead of resisting life's changes or forcing outcomes embrace life's natural rhythm. Recognise that not everything can be controlled, and this acceptance can ease the stress caused by unmet expectations.

Wu Wei: means effortless action. It does not mean inactivity but acting in alignment with flow of life. By avoiding struggle, resistance, stressing or trying to force outcomes , It teaches you acceptance, conserves energy and reduces mental strain.

Mindfulness and Present Moment Awareness. Be fully present in the moment without clinging to the past or worrying about the future. Stress often arises from overthinking. Taoism encourages quieting the mind and simply being.

Simplicity: Simplify your life by focusing on what truly matters. Detach from materialism and overcomplicated goals, which often leads to unnecessary stress. Taoism values simplicity and contentment.

Connection to Nature: Nature is seen as ultimate manifestation of the Tao. Spending time in nature helps reconnect with world's natural rhythm and help find peace amidst life's chaos.

The way to live Tao Life is to **Pause, Reflect, and** observe your thoughts and actions. Are you resisting something, are you forcing something, or are you not accepting something as it is? **Meditate to quiet the mind and** increase focus. **Go with the flow.** Practice flexibility and adjust your plans as circumstances change. **Detach From Outcomes.** Focus on the process rather than obsessing over results. **Live Simply,** declutter your mind, life and environment. Make it simple. Live simply. Living in Tao isn't about achieving perfection but about cultivating balance, inner peace, and alignment with life's natural rhythm. By letting go of unnecessary tension and embracing flow, you create space for stress to dissolve naturally.

PARADIGM SHIFT

The concept of a paradigm shift refers to a profound change in the fundamental approach or underlying assumptions about how we perceive and address situations. When applied to stress management, a paradigm shift involves changing our mindset and reaction to challenges, problems and issues.

The Traditional Approach: Resistance and Stress: In most cases, stress is triggered when we resist problems or unfavourable situations in life. Resistance arises because 1) We dislike the situation. 2) We want it to change immediately. 3) We feel threatened, triggering the fight-or-flight response.

The resistance, however, doesn't solve the problem; instead, it worsens our stress and clouds our judgement.

The Paradigm Shift: Acceptance and Response: The shift lies in moving from resistance to **acceptance.** Here's what happens when we embrace this new approach.

1) Acceptance reduces resistance: Acknowledging that problems and challenges are a natural part of life removes the emotional energy spent on resisting them. **2) Calmness replaces stress:** When we accept instead of resist, our emotional state becomes more stable, reducing fight-or-flight response. **3) Rational problem-solving emerges:** Acceptance creates mental clarity, allowing us to use our intellect and creativity to address the problem effectively.

Practical Application. To practice this paradigm shift:

1. **Reframe problems as challenges:** Instead of seeing a situation as a "problem," view it as an opportunity to grow, learn, or adapt.

2. **Pause and observe:** Take a step back to understand the situation objectively without an immediate emotional reaction.

3. **Focus on solutions, not resistance:** Use logic, experience, and resources to address the issue instead of dwelling on why it occurred.

4. **Develop a growth mindset:** Believe that you can learn and grow from challenges rather than being defeated by them. This shift does not make problems disappear, but it transforms your relationship with them, enabling you to manage stress more effectively. By practising this approach,

you align your energy towards constructive actions rather than destructive resistance

FIX THE ROOF

The concept of "Fix the Roof " is to address the main issue that is causing you stress instead of just getting stressed. It emphasises focusing your energy on solving the root cause of a problem. This is difficult because when there is a problem, there is a high chance that negative thoughts that we are having could be perceived as a threat, and our body could get stressed to fight or run, which may overwhelm our reasoning and could make us react to the problem, but failing to address the core issue can make the situation worse.

How to "Fix the Roof" and address the main issue:

- **Identify the root cause**

- Pinpoint what's truly causing your stress. Is it workload, lack of clarity, poor communications, unmet expectations, late hours, etc?

- Avoid focusing solely on immediate frustrations, dig deeper to uncover the underlying problems. For example: If you are stressed about tight deadlines, the real issue might be unrealistic timelines or inefficient processes.

- **Take Proactive Steps:**

- Break down the problem into manageable parts and address it one step at a time

- Replace passive worrying with constructive actions. For example, If finances are a source of stress, create a budget, reduce unnecessary expenses, or seek financial advice.

- **Focus on Solutions.**

- The natural tendency is to dwell on the problem, feeling bad about it or blaming someone for it, but this does not get solutions; instead of dwelling on the problem, find a way to fix it.

- Channel energy into actionable solutions. Example If team member's lack of collaboration is affecting your work, have a clear and respectful conversation to resolve the conflict.

- **Learn from the Experience.**

- Once you solve the problem, reflect on what you can do to prevent similar issues in the future.

- This might involve improving systems, learning new skills, creating a contingency fund or setting clearer boundaries. For example, if the job loss was a total surprise and caused you stress, it would help to have a contingency plan, contingency fund, a list of organisations and people you can reach, and an updated CV ready at all times.

- **Control What You Can, Let Go of What You Can't.**

- Some issues would be beyond our control. We may not be in control of the situation, but we can be in control of our response. Focus on what you can change instead of stressing about what you can't. For example, if the company's toxic work culture is the source of constant focus on trying to get a new job with an organisation with good work culture or find some new way to make money. Your priority is your well-being.

By "fixing the roof (addressing the main issue), you are resolving the source of stress rather than dealing with recurring symptoms. You feel empowered, as you are actively working towards a solution. Building resilience, knowing you can handle challenges constructively. This approach ensures that you are not just stressed about leaking roof but working out a more permanent solutions to prevent future leaks.

CHAPTER 7
STRATEGIES TO REDUCE STRESS

"The greatest weapon against stress is our ability to choose one thought over another."

Stress has become pervasive part of modern life, affecting our mental, emotional and physical well-being. In a fast-paced world filled with demand, deadlines, and distractions, handling stress is not just about finding relief in the moment but about using our intelligence to understand root causes of stress and adopting strategies to reduce it.

WORK STRESS

Work pressure: there is too much to do and too little time to do it. It is important to prioritise tasks; communication about priorities should be clear, as what may be a priority to you may not be a priority to your boss. Learn to delegate less priority work and establish a reporting system.

The 80/20 principle needs to be adopted; focus on the 20 percent of tasks that produce 80 percent of the results.

Time slots need to be allotted. Checking of mail and messaging could be slotted so that it does not interfere with other productive work. There is a study that indicates that if the mind is distracted, it takes 19 minutes to regain focus again. Avoid distractions. There are productivity techniques like Pomodoro and other techniques that can improve productivity.

Learn not to get provoked or instigated. Use the karma technique to avoid getting disturbed.

Learn to say "NO!" Set clear boundaries between work and personal life. Avoid getting influenced by people who have learnt the art of stretching two hours of work to twelve hours; they are insecure and pretend they are working hard. There are enough studies that state that the human brain cannot focus for more than six to eight hours; productivity actually decreases if you try to work more than the hour that you are productive. Rest and recuperation are required by the human brain to be more productive.

If you don't get time to exercise, then use lunchtime to walk. Use the gym near your office. Bad posture is creating pain. You can learn and do stretching exercises in your office using a chair, table, and wall. It will just take up to five minutes, but it will reduce your back, neck, and wrist pain. Take regular breaks. Power meditation or mindfulness of five minutes is a big help. Cool-down techniques are a big help to defuse stress.

Do talk. It is not easy to carry the burden alone. Have a buddy, a confidant, be in a team that

Support each other. Have a mentor; it helps to talk to a senior who has seen it all before.

It helps people to help as they feel good. It is human nature to help if help is asked for.

Do talk to your family. The families are the divine building block of the society. The family which shares are the family which cares.

Build an emergency fund, save, invest. Financial challenges put maximum pressure on expenses.

Continue even when inflow stops temporarily. Be curious, acquire more skill sets, and be on LinkedIn.

Join a support group, learn to manage stress, learn to like, even if you don't like to do so.

Reduce stress, allocate time to do what you enjoy, have a hobby, and also ensure that you sleep the hours that you need to sleep to feel rested.

FINANCIAL STRESS

These are some of the strategies suggested to reduce financial challenges.

Create a budget, track your expenses and income, figure out where you are spending, and identify areas where you can reduce expenses. Think about ways to increase your income. Online offers multiple opportunities to add to your income, which may include freelance work, coaching, consultancy, etc. Please check the company's policy before taking up online assignments.

Reduce debt. Pay down high-interest debts to reduce interest payments. Revolving credit in credit cards, interest-bearing personal loans, etc., can be consolidated. Paying off short-term loans with higher outflow and higher interest can be managed by long-term debt with lower outflow and lower interest.

Talking to bankers, creditors, etc., and renegotiating terms helps reduce pressure.

Online quick commerce sites offer better discounts. It may help to use them wisely to reduce costs.

It is believed that expense on our needs is hardly much. A major part of our expense is to fulfil our wants. It would help to reduce spending on wants and discretionary expense.

It would reduce pressure if the family chips in. Parents, spouses, and children can all supplement the income and reduce expenses.

Financial counsellors can help. An emergency fund is always a big help; it reduces pressure.

It helps to be sensible, rational, and intelligent and look out for out-of-the-box solutions. A finance specialist stuck in a large bank took a risk and shifted to a recently funded start-up as CFO with a huge sign-on bonus and a large package. A tech specialist, again stuck in a middle-level role, learnt the German Language and joined a company specialising in ERP in Germany on a big salary. Moving to that country reduced the cost of children's higher education, and his wife also got a role in a different software solutions company. Now, they commute to work in thirty minutes and get paid per hour instead of navigating traffic in Bangalore for two hours and getting paid less than half of what they are getting paid in Germany. Another person stuck in a low-paying accountant job is making big money teaching Excel to non-finance professionals online.

It is important to take care of self, exercise, meditation, mindfulness, sharing, spirituality, patience, perseverance, resilience, optimism, enthusiasm, determination, grit, etc., and reduce pressure.

Feel-good activities can reduce feel-bad pressure.

STRESS IN RELATIONSHIPS

Financial pressure is one of the main causes of stress in a relationship. It helps reduce financial pressure, and some of the strategies to reduce financial stress have been discussed earlier.

The ego is the big enemy of a relationship. Importance to self is pushing towards a different direction, and that leads to conflict. Ego makes it challenging to find a middle ground; there is no willingness to adjust or adapt. Arrogance kills the relationship.

Adjustment and adaptation issues can also put pressure on relationships. People have been brought up differently; they develop different habits. There could be a mismatch, and it helps to adjust and adapt. Finding a middle ground helps relationships.

The reality may not be as per expectation. Internally, people may be different from what they portray externally. It helps to accept reality and build on relationships.

Some couples who have shared an extended relationship believe that being a little blind to faults and a little deaf to complaints helps.

Physical affection, touch, hugs, kisses, sex, and spending quality time with each other strengthen the relationship.

The relationship is not only about seeing each other but also about doing many things together, enjoying shared interests, prioritising time for each other, and sharing common goals, which strengthens the relationship.

Communicate openly, share your feelings and concerns, listen actively, show appreciation, resolve conflicts quickly, support each other, forget and forgive, move forward, avoid blame, criticism, invest in building a relationship. If issues persist, it helps to have couple counselling.

HASSLES, IRRITATIONS IN LIFE

In India, there is a clan called Sholagas that whips themselves to reduce their problems. You may find it funny, but the fact is we lash ourselves when we get stressed. By self-inflicting wounds on ourselves, we are not reducing what is bothering us. It is believed that 50 percent of the stress we have is because of little things in life. You would have experienced that you are quick to get stressed, and it takes time to bounce back. It takes time for the heart to slow down, blood pressure to reduce, muscles to relax, irritation to reduce, etc. In modern life, there could be constant stressors. The air conditioner may not be cooling, water may be dripping from the tap, it may be raining or snowing, there could be a bad traffic jam, there could be bad drivers on the road, you may be late, your flight could be delayed, the mobile signal may be weak, your computer is unresponsive, your boss is in a bad mood, the kids are irritating, you could be irritated by a pesky call, there could be a million things that could be happening which may hassle you or irritate you, but these are not threats to your well-being. They are little things in life that are not the way you would like them to be. Getting stressed by the little things will not make the stressor go away but could build up cortisol, the stress hormone, which may create imbalances in your body. Why harm your body? By harming your body, you are not solving the problem, and the stressor is not in your control. You whip yourself up because that is what happens automatically, but that is not helping us. Our lower brain activates the automatic animal reaction that is present in us, like a bad habit. We must reduce our bad habits by being more aware, exerting more willpower to control ourselves, accept hassles, irritation, and little things in life as part and parcel of our life. They are not in our control, and we must control our urge to react to them.

STRESS AWARENESS

Recognising how stress manifests in your body and mind and then taking proactive steps to manage stress can reduce stress. Awareness of stress enables the adoption of proactive steps to control stress reactions. First, in detail, know stress symptoms: -

i.   **Physical signs:** When your body activates a "fight-or-flight response. This reaction can cause noticeable changes, such as: -

- Shallow, rapid breathing as your body tries to take in more oxygen.

- An increased heart rate as your body prepares for quick action.

- Muscle tension, often in areas like the neck, shoulders, or jaw.

- Stomach issues, which can range from nausea to cramps or digestion problems.

- Headache or a sensation of head fog, where you feel unfocused or disconnected.

- Sleep problems, where you may struggle to fall asleep, wake up frequently or feel restless.

- Panic attacks, which can include intense feelings of fear, a racing heart and sweating.

ii. **Emotional Signs:** Stress often affects your emotions, making it challenging to stay calm and balanced. Emotional stress indicators may include.

- Feeling of fear or anxiety, where one worries about things more than usual.

- Anger, aggression, or irritability, where one feels unusually snappy or frustrated.

- A sense of being overwhelmed, as though one can't handle what's on a plate.

- Restlessness and mood swings, where mood shifts quickly and unpredictably.

- Difficulty concentrating, a sense of distraction.

- A tendency to withdraw socially or feel disconnected from others.

iii. **Mental Signs:** Stress can interfere with clear thinking and focus. These mental signs include.

- Persistent worry, where one's mind keeps returning to certain thoughts or fears.

- Confusion or memory lapses, where it's difficult to remember things or think clearly.

- Racing thoughts, where one's mind jumps quickly from one idea to another.

- Trouble making decisions, as it is hard to evaluate choices.

- Negative thinking patterns, where one tends to focus on the worst-case scenario.

- Mental fatigue, where thinking or focusing feels like it requires extra effort.

- Difficulty relaxing even in calm environments.

iv. **Behavioural Signs**: Stress can impact how you behave or react in everyday situations. These behaviours include:

- Changes in appetite, where one may eat much more or much less than usual.

- Sleep disturbances, like sleeping too little or too much or having disrupted sleep.

- Becoming preoccupied with worries or stressors.

- Increased use of substances like alcohol, cigarettes or even drugs as a coping mechanism

- Procrastination, avoiding tasks, or putting off responsibilities.

- Avoidance behaviours, where one tries to avoid people or situations.

DEFUSE STRESS

To defuse stress means to "remove the fuse" – disconnecting the trigger that causes stress. Stress often stems from negative thoughts, which the brain perceives as threats, activating the body's fight-or-flight response. As psychologist Willam James said, "The *greatest weapon humans have against stress is their ability to choose one thought over another*" By replacing negative thoughts with positive or neutral ones, we can alter our response to stress. Additional techniques to defuse stress include:

- **Cool Down:** Take deep breaths or step away momentarily.

- **Reverse Counting:** Slowly count backwards to regain focus.

- **Break:** Take a short mental or physical break.

- **Labelling:** Identify and label stressful thoughts.

- **Cue Words:** Use positive words or phrases to ground self.

- **Self-Talk:** Encourage self with reassuring thoughts.

- **Visualisation**: Imagine a cam place or positive outcome.

- **Mindful Awareness: Stay present, noticing thoughts and sensations without judgement**.

BE HUMAN

Being human means approaching life's challenges with rationality, resilience and adaptability. It's about using our intellect to analyse and creatively solve problems rather than reacting with fear, stress or avoidance. To "be human" is to.

i. Recognise that lifestyle threats are not life-threatening.

ii. Respond with reason instead of reacting with stress or anger.

iii. Embrace acceptance and adaptability over resistance.

iv. Adjust, adapt, and be open to change.

v. Take control rather than feeling overwhelmed.

vi. View stress as a mindset; if you choose not to get stressed, you will feel at ease.

vii. Be proactive and prepared rather than shocked.

viii. Remember that life's challenges are temporary and bring opportunities.

ix. Tap into our unique human qualities, like our spirit, creativity, and sense of purpose, to overcome adversity.

Ultimately, being human involves cultivating a growth mindset, relying on support systems, and embracing the opportunities that life offers. Being human can help reduce stress.

BE SRI

Being 'SRI' is a concept based on the acronym SRI: Sensible, Rational, Intelligent - qualities that embody our higher human nature. Rooted in both Eastern spiritualism and practical wisdom 'SRI' serves as a reminder to act from a place of patience, resilience and reason rather than reacting impulsively in stressful situations; saying "Be SRI" can be a cue to handle challenges thoughtfully while keeping control over emotions and staying focused on the bigger purpose, rather than responding with anger, frustration or stress. This simple reminder encourages us to rise above instinctive reactions, embracing a calm, enlightened approach to life's daily hassles and stresses.

HAVE HIGHER PURPOSE IN LIFE

Having a higher purpose in life provides a sense of direction, meaning and fulfilment, which can significantly reduce stress. A higher purpose helps us to see beyond immediate stressors, focusing on long-term goals and values rather than short-term challenges. When we are connected to a meaningful purpose, we are more likely to face obstacles with a positive mindset and bounce back from setbacks.

A clear purpose acts as a compass, helping prioritise what's truly important and letting go of unnecessary worries. Knowing that we are working towards something meaningful can foster a sense of peace, gratitude and contentment, reducing anxiety and restlessness.

The Eastern spiritual philosophy emphasises that the higher purpose of human life extends beyond basic animal instincts like survival and reproduction. Here's a breakdown of this philosophy.

Be Human: Cultivate reason, emotional control, and self -mastery. Eastern beliefs stress that true humanity involves controlling our responses rather than letting impulses dictate actions. Emotions like fear, anger and anxiety can be managed allowing individuals to respond rationally to stress.

Live Life: Life includes both highs and lows. Accepting this ebb and flow with resilience and equanimity is essence of life. Life's journey encompasses successes, failures and challenges, the purpose is to live life fully without surrendering to hardship prematurely.

Be Happy: As Dalai Lama suggests, happiness is central purpose. This involves cultivating a positive state of mind, finding joy in both small pleasures and profound experiences. Happiness varies but remains a personal choice, independent of external conditions. One can be happy in all conditions, for any reason, in every season, if one chooses to be happy.

Be Useful: Humans are interconnected and meant to serve each other. You give, you get. Each individual has unique talents and passion, skill, education and experience that contribute to the society. The act of giving and being of service fulfils a meaningful aspect of life's purpose.

Be Responsible: Personal responsibility for one's body, mind and emotions is essential. This means nurturing self-respect, avoiding self-criticism and fulfilling duties oneself and others who are dependent on us

PROBLEMS IN LIFE ARE SPIRITUAL TEST

Problems in life are spiritual test is rooted in the belief that life's challenges are designed to test and refine the human spirit. According to this belief, the soul undergoes an ongoing journey through various forms of life., reincarnating in may bodies across different life cycles.

Being born in human form represents a significant stage in this journey - a final stage where the soul faces the ultimate tests to achieve spiritual maturity.

In this human form, people inherit animal instincts, such as fight-or-flight response that triggers stress when they sense danger. However, humans have also been gifted with higher reasoning, self-awareness, and the ability to manage these instincts. This belief posits that problems serve as opportunities to see whether the soul can transcend its animalistic impulses and respond with calm, reasoned human qualities like patience, resilience, faith and perseverance.

Each problem encountered is seen as a test: does the individual react impulsively, as animals do, with stress, fear or aggression? Or do they respond with human virtues, maintaining calm, control, and thoughtful responses? If the person defaults to instinctive reactions, becoming overwhelmed or stressed, they fail the test, showing the soul is still operating at lower, animalistic level.

However, if they pass the test - staying composed, rational, and enduring - they demonstrate qualities of the human spirit and advance spiritually. According to this view, souls that fail the test will continue to cycle through life and death until they learn to respond as humans. But those who succeed are believed to break free from this cycle, achieving what Hinduism calls moksha and Buddhism calls *nirvana,* a liberation from the cycle of birth and rebirth.

This belief can provide comfort, as it reframes life's difficulties as meaningful tests rather than random misfortunes. Seeing problems as a chance to grow and strengthen human virtues encourages a mindset that can reduce stress and promote spiritual development.

ACCEPTANCE

Acceptance is a powerful concept that revolves around the idea of embracing reality as it is rather than fighting against it. It means acknowledging that certain situations, losses, or disappointments are beyond our control and that life doesn't always unfold according to our expectations. This willingness to accept things as they are without denial, guilt, or resistance is essential for mental peace and well-being. When people struggle with acceptance, they often find themselves in a cycle of denial, guilt, or pretending that everything is as they wish it to be. This resistance creates stress because it's an attempt to control the uncontrollable or rewrite reality. Such resistance triggers the body's fight-or-flight response, a survival mechanism that produces stress hormones, increasing physical and mental strain. This stress can further worsen the situation, compounding the sense of imbalance and creating health and emotional challenges.

Acceptance doesn't mean giving up or surrendering in a passive way. Rather, it means acknowledging that a situation is real and needs to be faced, however uncomfortable that might be. By accepting, we reduce inner resistance and free mental energies, allowing us to use our intellect, reason and resilience more effectively to respond to challenges. When we don't waste energy fighting against what's beyond our control, we gain the clarity to explore solutions, adapt and make thoughtful responses. Acceptance helps us shift from expecting life to adjust to us to adapting ourselves to life's inevitable ups and downs. This outlook enables a broader emotional bandwidth to deal with setbacks, failures, successes and joys. By embracing both the positive and the negative, we build a balanced perspective, allowing us to manage stress, grow from experience, and continue moving forward with a healthier, more adaptable mindset.

HAND IT OVER TO GOD

"Hand it over to God" is a spiritual and mental practice of surrendering control over aspects of life that are beyond your power to change. It is rooted in the belief that a higher power, or God, has a bigger plan which will guide you through challenges when the time is right. This practice involves letting go of resistance, fear and anxiety and trusting that things will unfold as they are meant to.

When faced with uncertainty or situations where the solutions seem out of reach, "handing it over to God" encourages

"Surrender" acknowledges that not everything is within your control and lets go of the need to force outcomes. **"Trust" means** believing in the wisdom and guidance of a higher power, trusting that it has your best interests at heart. **"Patience"** means allowing time for things to unfold as they should without letting stress or anxiety dominate your present." Faith" means having confidence that " God" will bring clarity, peace, and solutions at the right moment. "Acceptance" **means** embracing life as it is and learning to adapt to what comes your way without resistance. This mindset can help you find inner peace by shifting the focus from what you can't control to what you can, which is your response, attitude and faith. It's a way of aligning yourself with the flow of life rather than fighting against it.

TAKE UP THE CHALLENGE

Taking a challenge is about transforming how we respond to difficult situations. When we see a negative or demanding situation as a challenge rather than a threat, we can trigger eustress or positive stress. Eustress energises us, boosting motivation, alertness and resilience without invoking the intense fear or survival responses associated with negative stress.

Viewing a problem as a challenge means we perceive ourselves as capable and in control. This perspective can spark an adrenaline rush, which enhances our focus and readiness. Unlike when we're fearful or defensive, seeing a challenge fosters a sense of purpose and a state of flow, allowing us to respond with clarity rather than fight-or-flight rather than fight-or-flight. Our body recognises that, while the situation is tough, there's no immediate risk to our lives. This lets us engage calmly, with energy and focus, which is essential in the modern world, where success often relies on critical thinking and problem-solving.

The body's survival instinct is a powerful, hard-wired response. When threatened, it reacts automatically to stress and shuts down non-essential processes, which could hinder complex thinking. However, by consciously interpreting a difficult situation as a challenge rather than a threat, we signal to our brain that survival responses aren't necessary. This approach lets us harness the power of good stress, empowering us to navigate challenges thoughtfully, building resilience and a proactive mindset.

WHAT YOU CAN SAY TO SELF TO REDUCE STRESS

Here are examples of self-talk statements you can use to reduce stress.

To Calm Self:

- *I am safe right now: I can handle this.*

- *The situation is temporary; this feeling is temporary, and this will all pass.*

- *I can breathe deeply and let go of tension.*

- *I don't have to have all the answers right now.*

To Reframe Negative Thoughts:

- *I am doing the best I can with what I have.*

- *One setback doesn't define me.*

- *I can learn and grow from this experience.*

- *It is okay to make mistakes; I am human.*

To Build Confidence:

- *I have faced challenges before, and I can overcome them, too.*

- *I am capable, strong, and resourceful.*

- *I have the tools to figure this out.*

- *I trust myself to make good decisions*

To Manage Overwhelm:

- *I'll focus on one step at a time.*

- *I don't need to do everything at once.*

- *I can prioritise and let go of what is not urgent.*

- *It's Okay to take a break and recharge.*

To Stay Positive:

- *There is good in this moment; I just need to find it.*

- *I am grateful for the things I have accomplished.*

- *This is a challenge, but it's an opportunity to grow.*

- *Every small step forward is progress.*

For Motivation:

- *I have what it takes to move forward.*

- *I can turn stress into energy by taking it on as a challenge to achieve my goals.*

- *I am in control of my response to this situation.*

- *I am bigger than my problems.*

To End the Day on a Positive Note.

- *I did my best today in the circumstances I was in, and that's enough.*

- *I am proud of the effort I put in.*

- *Tomorrow is a new day with new opportunities.*

- *I am letting go of today's stress and choosing rest.*

By repeating these statements, you can rewire your thought patterns, reduce stress, and cultivate a more positive and balanced mindset.

VENKY AND HIS FEELINGS

Venky was a highly accomplished tech executive who worked at one of the four big tech companies in Bengaluru. On the surface, he had everything: a six-figure salary, a luxurious apartment and recognition in his field. One day, Venkat happened to see a video on YouTube by a former successful tech executive who spoke about the lack of a career for executives who had crossed forty years of age in the tech industry. Venkat was forty-five years of age. In the recent past, the projects that were coming his way had reduced. He was consumed by insecurity, anxiety and stress. Venkat dreaded waking up each morning. Traffic was horrendous, meetings felt like torture, deadlines loomed like dark clouds, and the endless grind left him drained. His health began to deteriorate - he had frequent headaches, insomnia and even bouts of chest pain. His personal life also suffered; the distance between him and his wife grew wider, and his young daughter barely got to see him.

One evening, after a particularly gruelling day, Venkat found himself staring at his reflection in the office washroom mirror. He hardly recognised the weary, joyless man looking back. That night, as he lay awake, he made a decision that changed his life forever: *If I can't change my circumstances, I will change how I feel about them. I will enjoy my work.*

Venkat began his journey by revisiting why he entered the tech industry in the first place. He remembered his engineering college days; he was passionate about technology's power to solve real-world problem's. Somewhere along he had lost that spark. He had been avoiding upgrading self because he felt he was old to learn new tricks but he started reading about Artificial Intelligence and was enchanted about the power of AI to solve real world problem. His interest grew.

Venkat started small, each morning before diving into his emails, he spent 10 minutes journaling about 3 things that he appreciated about his work. Some days it was the impact of the product his team built; other days it was appreciation of the lifestyle that his work was providing. Over time, these moments of gratitude began to add up.

Next, he made an effort to find meaning in his day-to-day tasks. Instead of seeing his role as just managing projects, he reframed it as empowering his team to innovate and succeed. He became genuinely curious about their ideas, took time to celebrate small wins, and began to view challenges as opportunities for growth. The change was gradual but profound. Venkat's new perspective reduced his stress levels, and his health started to improve. He began practising mindfulness and took short breaks during the day to recharge. At home, his transformation didn't go unnoticed; his wife saw a lighter, more present version of her husband. Venkat made it a point to end work on time at least twice a week to have dinner with his family. On weekends, he started taking his daughter to Cubbon Park, strengthening their bonds.

Venkat's new found passion and positivity also had ripple effect on his career. His team noticed his enthusiasm and responded in kind, producing some of their best work. One of their projects - a ground breaking AI-based solution for one of the world's largest health care programmes caught the attention of the company's leadership. Within a year, Venkat was promoted to a global leadership role, overseeing innovation across multiple regions. The success was sweeter because it no longer came at the cost of his health or relationship.

Venkat's story is a testament to the power of perspective. By deliberately choosing to like what he did, he not only transformed his career but also enriched his life. Today, Venkat is a sought-after speaker, sharing his journey with others who feel trapped by their circumstances. His mantra? *"You don't have to wait for the perfect job to find joy in your work. Sometimes, the biggest transformation happens when you change the way you see what's already in front of you."*

TWENTY-FIVE THINGS TO LET GO TO REDUCE STRESS

1. **Perfectionism** - Embrace progress over perfection.

2. Need **For Control** - Accept that not everything is within your power.

3. **Fear of Failure** - See failure as an opportunity to grow and learn.

4. **People-pleasing** - Prioritise your own needs and boundaries.

5. **Comparison** - Focus on your own journey, not others.

6. **Negative self-talk** - Speak to yourself with kindness and encouragement.

7. **Overthinking** - Trust your decisions and stop replaying scenarios in your head.

8. **Unrealistic expectations** - Set achievable goals for yourself and others.

9. **Holding grudges** - Forgive and let go for your own peace of mind.

10. **Seeking external validation** - Believe in your worth without needing approval.

11. **Need to be always right** - Value understanding over winning arguments.

12. **Dwelling on the past** - Focus on what you can change in the present.

13. **Fear of the unknown** - Embrace uncertainty as part of life.

14. **Guilt over taking breaks** - Rest is productive. Allow yourself to recharge

15. **Believing you must do everything** - Ask for help when required.

16. **Thinking stress is unavoidable** - Shift your mindset and practice stress management.

17. **Assuming worst-case scenario** - Replace catastrophising thoughts with rational thinking.

18. **Overcommitment** - Learn to say no and respect your limits.

19. **Toxic relationship** - Distance yourself from people who drain your energy.

20. **Lack of sleep** - Prioritise rest and create sleep hygiene.

21. **Excessive screen time** - Switch off from work and spend less time on social media.

22. **Procrastination** - Take small steps to tackle tasks now.

23. **Negative News** - Let Go of the temptation to seek negative news.

24. **Expectations** - Let go of the expectation and accept the reality.

25. **Resistance** – Let go of resistance if things are not as to your liking. Accept destiny.

"TWENTY-FIVE" WAYS TO UPLIFT YOUR MOOD

Mood uplifters reduce stress by triggering the release of positive chemicals in the brain, like dopamine, endorphins, serotonin and oxytocin, which can counteract stress response, leading to feelings of relaxation, happiness and more positive outlook. Here are "twenty-five" easy ways that you can uplift your mood.

1. **Practice Gratitude** – Make a list of things that you're thankful for daily. Gratitude shifts focus to positives in life.

2. **Meditate** – Spend 10 minutes focusing on your breath to clear your mind and reduce stress.

3. **Exercise** – Physical activity releases feel-good hormones, boosting your mood.

4. **Listen to Music** – Play your favourite songs to uplift your spirit.

5. **Spent Time in Nature** – Go for a walk or sit in the park to feel connected and refreshed.

6. **Journal Your Thoughts** – Write down your emotions to process them and find clarity.

7. **Indulge in Hobby** – Do something that you love: painting, reading, cooking, gardening, etc.

8. **Try Something New** – Explore new activities or places to bring excitement to the routine.

9. **Connect with Loved Ones** – Call or meet up with family or friends to uplift you.

10. **Treat Yourself** – Buy yourself a small gift or indulge in your favourite food.

11. **Watch a Comforting Movie or Show** – Revisit something that brings joy and relaxation.

12. **Practice Self-Care** – Enjoy a relaxing bath, massage, or simply rest.

13. **Laugh** – Watch a comedy or recall funny memories to instantly brighten your mood.

14. **Set Small Goals** – Achieving even small goals gives a sense of accomplishment.

15. **Do Yog Nidra** – Relaxing yourself through Yog Nidra uplifts your mood.

16. **Volunteer or Help Someone** – Helping others gives a sense of purpose and fulfilment.

17. **Hug** – Hugging someone releases feel-good hormones.

18. **Read an inspiring story** – Reading an inspiring story of achievers inspires and feels good.

19. **Play** – Playing, having fun, laughing, and enjoying makes you feel good.

20. **Dance Freely** – Dancing freely to the rhythm of your favourite music makes you feel good.

21. **Spent Time with Pets** – If you have a pet, play or cuddle - they are great mood boosters.

22. **Declutter Your Mind** – Practice "brain dump" write and delete what is not required.

23. **Sleep** – A good sleep, a rested mind and body, feels great.

24. **Compliment Self** – Acknowledge your achievements and strengths. Be good to yourself.

25. **Positive Journal** – Maintain a journal with content that makes you happy, joyful, and feel good.

EXPECTATION

What is stress? What is the gap between reality and expectation? People put a lot of pressure on themselves by having high expectations and are disappointed when reality does not meet their expectations. People have big expectations, *"I expect my spouse to be this way," "I expect my child to score 90%," "I expect no pressure in the office,"*

"I expect people to respect me," "I expect to be paid 50% more for my work," "I expected to be promoted," etc. If things are not as per their expectations, they get upset, angry, stressed, sulk, fight, get hostile, are bitter, resentful, lose their sleep, and lose their health. That creates problems for them.

We can set expectations and work hard towards achieving them. The actual outcomes are often beyond our control. Focusing on effort rather than outcome can help reduce stress and anxiety. Bhagavad Gita, a renowned scripture in Hinduism, which could have been written more than 5000 years ago, has the following quote: *"You have the right to perform your duty. You are doing your karma, but you are not entitled to the fruits of the action as it is not in your control. Considering yourself to be the cause of the results of your activity is an error. Winning or losing is not in your hands. Do your duty without expectation or fear of failure."* A lot of stressful situations are created because reality does not meet our expectations. We did not get the job we expected, and the spouse we married was not as we expected. Work is not going as we expected. Be rational. How is getting upset, angry, or disappointed going to help the situation? By getting emotional and stressed, we are only creating more problems for ourselves. Why not accept reality and use your intellect for betterment?

PERCEPTION

You are getting stressed because your lower brain is automatically perceiving that you are under threat or there is a danger to your life. If you analyse the reason why you are getting stressed, it would be some problem or challenge in life which is not a threat to your life but some issues that can, at maximum, create some hardship, discomfort, or inconvenience for a short period of time. The problem that you are facing will not kill you, but the automatic stress that is being triggered may harm you in the long term. It would help to be human, sensible, rational, and intelligent; consider the problem to be a challenge and ask yourself questions like, "How can I solve this problem?" "What am I doing about what is bothering me?" *"How can I reduce this stress?"* etc. could help you reduce stress.

If you need to be perfect, you create space for growth, joy, and a life free from unnecessary stress. After all, its our imperfections that makes us human and ultimately, makes life worth living.

HOPE

A spiritual person may be more likely to be at peace with themselves. There is a high level of acceptance because of the belief that God has willed it that way, and the problems and challenges in life become tests of the human spirit. Faith, hope, and trust build resilience because the belief in support from the all-powerful makes everyone stronger. Hope is of incredible psychological strength. In the famous experiment called the Hope Experiment, Dr. Carl Richter of Johns Hopkins University conducted two experiments. In the first experiment, he dropped an unsuspecting set of rats into a bucket filled with water. Rats are normally known to be good swimmers, but these rats, when they suddenly found themselves in a difficult situation, panicked and began to paddle furiously. They went berserk and drowned in fifteen minutes. When the experiment was repeated with a second set of rats, the initial reaction was the same, but they were picked up, comforted, and then dropped back into the water. When the rats got to hope that they would be rescued, they swam and swam for sixty hours, which is four thousand times longer than the first instance where they had panicked. Belief in a higher power reduces stress.

A THERAPIST CAN HELP REDUCE STRESS

Therapists are educated, trained, and experienced to handle stress. They can help you understand why you feel stressed, identify the triggers for stress, and recognise negative thought patterns and harmful behaviour patterns. They can assist you with coping and problem-solving strategies, help you relax, and answer many of your questions. They can help you feel better and enable you to look at your issues from a different perspective. Mental health challenges are also health challenges. We are comfortable seeking treatment for physical health issues; similarly, we should be comfortable seeking treatment for mental health issues.

CBT CAN HELP REDUCE STRESS

Cognitive Behaviour Therapy is a talking therapy based on the concept of the connection between our thoughts, feelings, and actions. CBT helps identify negative thought patterns and tries to establish their link to why you are feeling the way you are feeling and why you are behaving the way you are behaving. CBT helps you to change your negative thought patterns, which are responsible for trapping you in a negative cycle. CBT could help you deal with a complex problem by breaking it down into more manageable, actionable parts so that you are not overwhelmed by the problem.

DON'T BE TOO CRITICAL OF SELF

Don't be too critical of yourself; be wary of making statements like, "I am no good," "My family hates me," or "My office hates me." "I can't do anything right," "I am a failure," "I wish I was more like him or her," and other similar critical words. They create stress and may lead to depression. It is human nature to forget the thousands of rights we have done but remember one wrong. This is because of evolutionary reasons. When humans were just like any other animal, one wrong could mean death. So, in our lower brain, a wrong is perceived so negatively. But as humans, a wrong may mean learning, a mistake that helps you grow. There is already pressure on you; why double the pressure by being critical of yourself?

LABELLING OF THOUGHTS CAN HELP REDUCE STRESS

Negative thoughts could make you feel negative and trigger stress. Many times, you may have an awareness of thoughts triggering you, and you can stop the thoughts by reminding yourself, "Don't be an animal; be human." You can also say "STOP" or "Quiet" to your thoughts. This trick works because our mind can only think of one thought at a given time. If you keep on saying "quiet, quiet" to your mind, the mind has no choice but to remain quiet because it cannot have another thought while it is handling one thought. Try this technique and enjoy the feeling of peacefulness and calm when the mind becomes quiet.

DELETING THOUGHTS CAN HELP REDUCE STRESS

In modern life, there can be many distractions. There could be news, emails, messages, comments, incidents, etc., that don't add value to our lives but can occupy mind space. Deleting thoughts that are not required can clear the mind space they occupy. Once you are mindful of these thoughts and consciously delete them, you may experience some load being lifted from your mind.

STOPPING RUMINATION CAN HELP REDUCE STRESS

Rumination is repeatedly thinking about or focusing on negative thoughts and emotions. It is like our thoughts are in an endless loop, significantly increasing our stress levels. While there may be negative situations, thinking about the same thing, again and again, will not solve or cope with the situation; instead, it will increase your stress because every time you get stressed, you are adding stress hormones to your system, and they keep piling up. Telling your mind, "Thank you for making me alert, but now stop reminding or nagging about the same thing," could help.

CHALLENGING THOUGHTS CAN HELP REDUCE STRESS

Challenging thoughts and reframing them into a more balanced and realistic perspective can reduce stress, anxiety, and depression. As repeated earlier, modern-day threats are not a threat to life. There are studies that state that ninety-seven percent of the time, what we are anxious about does not happen, or we handle them better than expected. All problems and challenges are temporary, and they pass. The maximum that happens is that for a temporary period of time, they may create some discomfort. Our lower brain has a tendency to overreact; it is designed to believe that the challenges we are facing are a threat to life that may kill us. That perception makes us fight or run, get stressed, trigger anxiety, depression, etc. It would help us to be more sensible and rational, use our intelligence, and be more realistic and balanced. It would help challenge and reframe our thoughts. For example, if you have made a mistake or you have failed and you are getting very stressed and anxious about that, it would help to tell your brain, "Please don't overreact; it is just a mistake or a failure which can happen in life. That is how people learn by making mistakes. I will learn from my mistakes and failures and not repeat those mistakes next time." The animal brain in us is emotional and tends to overreact. It helps to challenge thoughts and make them more practical and realistic.

FORGIVE AND FORGET

Somebody has done wrong to us; some things have been unfair and unjust. It is natural to feel negative about that person or thing. There are going to be automatic negative thoughts that will constantly disturb you, putting you in a state of arousal. You could be constantly agitated, and the slightest provocation could cause a flare-up. There could be constant stress and tension, which would constantly cause discomfort in our bodies. While we are punishing our body, the person or the things that are causing us stress are unaffected. Not only are we victims of wrong, but we unknowingly punish ourselves. Being the higher person in such a situation helps; the bigger purpose in life is not to hurt our bodies but to be happy. Forgiving and forgetting to reduce stress.

MONKEY MIND

The Buddhist Monks call the mind a monkey mind because the nature of our mind is to wander, be curious, get distracted, jump around, have thoughts, be fearful, be negative, etc. It is believed that our mind can have about 60,000 thoughts in a day; 95% of these thoughts can be useless or repetitive. The brain weighs around 2% of our body but consumes 20% of the energy required by the body. It is constantly generating automatic thoughts, and therefore, our brain is tired when we want to use it for useful thinking. Thoughts also trigger stress. We feel good when we have good thoughts and feel bad when we have bad thoughts. We get stressed when we have threatening thoughts. Unregulated thoughts can harm us, so there is a need to regulate our thoughts. We need to become more aware of our thoughts. If there are useful thoughts, even if they are negative, we can say thanks to our mind, noting that thought. Why? The reason is that if we let our brain automatically process negative thoughts, it may perceive those thoughts as a physical threat and trigger a physical response, urging our body to fight or run, causing stress. It would help to reframe the thought. It would help to tell our primal brain not to react like an animal but to acknowledge that I feel there may be some threat to my job and that I should plan my response just in case money stops coming in, etc.

If there are useless thoughts, it is better to recognise them and delete them. Why waste energy and make our brains tired? If there are thoughts about people who are not in our control, it is better not to respond to them. Stop the thoughts that speak negatively to us, affecting our confidence and self-esteem. Stop those thoughts that compare us with others. Stop thoughts of regret, grudge, bereavement, mistake, failure. Why whip ourselves by thinking about past negative situations? How is that going to help us? We also need to avoid stimulants that would unnecessarily excite the monkey mind in us; that may include negative news, politics, gossip, scandals, WhatsApp universities, etc. The less distracted we are from what is good for us, the less stressed we are. The better it would be for us. It is the duty of our mind to make us aware, alert, cautious, and warn us, but it is our duty to be the master of our mind and make the mind our servant, not make our mind our master and react without using our mind. Control your monkey mind to reduce stress.

BEING PREPARED CAN HELP REDUCE STRESS

For an extended period of time in our lives, we meet the same people, do the same job, and have similar routines. We may face similar disagreements, the same friction points, similar types of clients, similar routines, etc. If we are surprised or unprepared, it could trigger stress within us. But if that pattern repeats, it is not a surprise. It helps to have our own 'standard operating procedure'. That is to say, 'I will avoid saying something to my spouse/boss/family, etc., that triggers stress.' If the next time this negative thought comes, this is how I will respond. 'Why did I respond like an animal and get stressed? If the next time this incident occurs, I will respond this way.' You can prepare your standard operating procedure so that you are not taken by surprise, and you are prepared with your response.

CHAPTER 8
TECHNIQUES TO MANAGE STRESS

"The problem is outside; by stressing, you are beating yourself self-inside."

– Guru

Managing stress is essential because unchecked stress can have significant negative impacts on both physical and mental health. Chronic stress increases the risks of issues like anxiety, depression, heart disease, high blood pressure and weakened immunity. It can impair focus, decision making and productivity, leading to burnout and diminished quality of life. Stress also affects relationships, as irritability and emotional exhaustion can strain interactions with others. By managing stress effectively, we can improve overall well-being, enhance resilience, maintain healthier relationships, and foster a more positive outlook on life. Managing stress is a vital step in achieving balance, fulfilment and long-term health.

4-7-8 BREATHING TECHNIQUE

is a simple technique that can help you relax and relieve stress. Our body gets stressed so that it can fight or run. That requires an increase in blood pressure, which in turn requires an increase in heart rate, which requires an increase in breath rate, and in the 4-7-8 breathing technique, you reduce the breath rate. The technique is to breathe in through your nose to count to 4, then hold the breath to count to 7 and finally release the breath through your mouth to count to 8. In this technique, you are holding and exhaling your breath for a period longer than you breathe in, thus automatically reducing your breath rate, thus reducing your heart rate and blood pressure.

REDUCE OVERTHINKING

It is very common to find people overthinking, and that leads to anxiety and stress. People are putting themselves under intense scrutiny. There are constant thoughts about what I said was the correct thing to do, what others would be thinking, and why that person is ignoring me; the focus is on I, Me, Myself, which leads to a kind of introversion and constant friction to free flow. People are making self-miserable, to manage to overthink, it would help to be aware of your thoughts, stop scrutinising, stop being perfectionist, stop focusing on what others would, people who matter have no time for gossip people who don't matter have all the time for gossip, it makes sense to spend more time with people who matter and do what matters. If you feel you are getting overpowered by obsessive thoughts or there is a constant rumination of past events, uncertainty, fears, and anxieties, it helps to write to journal your thoughts or write dairy. Talk it out. Being busy and having no time for obsessive thoughts helps. But it does so happen that you may be busy in the morning. It is at night that this thought comes to disturb your sleep. Closing shop is stopping indulging in mental activity that makes the neurons in your brain go into a frenzy. Distracting from oneself, reading, having family time, and maintaining a circadian rhythm, such as sleeping on time, all help to reduce overthinking and manage stress.

EVENTS NOT IN OUR CONTROL

The other major reason for stress is that people want to control what is not in their control and get upset, feel anxious, and get stressed. The jobs may not be in your control, the kids may not be in your control, the economy may not be in your control, and changes may not be in your control. It is high time that we reduced the need to be in control and accepted situations that were not in our control. Do not expect everything to be black and white, but accept the grey. I have met many people who are stressed because their position in life is not commensurate with their academic excellence or their kids are not as successful as they are. They have many whys and whys that are unexplainable; they are not only stressed because of their challenge. In addition, because they are stressed, they face more challenges. Nearly a hundred years ago, the prayer for serenity captured it well. *"God grant me the serenity to accept things I cannot change, Courage to change the things I can, and Wisdom to know the difference."* Recognise what you can't control, accept, and let go of resistance. Focus on what you can control. Concentrate on the present rather than worrying about the past or future. Do your duty, and don't get attached to outcomes or expectations. Have faith that God has the right plan for you. Have gratitude and focus on good things in your life rather than making yourself miserable by focusing on what is not there. Happiness, Peace and Calm within is the greatest of all success; change your perspective. Manage your stress.

SAY NO

If stress is not helping you, why get stressed? Because stress could actually harm you. Blood pressure, diabetes, heart issues, and stomach acidity can be related to stress. So, next time something irritates you or stresses you, say, **"STOP STRESS."** I don't want diabetes, high blood pressure, heart attack, etc. The fear of acquiring stress-related diseases may overpower your urge to get upset or irritated.

TRICKING THE MIND

Tricking the mind could also help you manage stress. That is, when you feel stress is triggered, you can deliberately change your thoughts. Think about somebody or something that makes you feel good. Stress is triggered by negative thoughts. By changing your thoughts, you can change your response.

VISUALISATION

It is a good technique to manage stress by imagining yourself to be in a serene, calm, tranquil scene, being relaxed and happy only if it is in your mind; it distracts your mind and tricks the brain, triggers positive thoughts and perks up your mood. The mental break enables your body to relax, cortisol, the stress hormones are reduced, and the feel-good hormones are increased. Athletes use visualisation to tap into their imaginative power to create desired feelings and outcomes. Visualisation can be used along with breathing techniques to relax and manage your stress.

THOUGHT CLEARANCE

Your unnecessary thoughts trigger stress. If you feel stressed, take a small break. Identify the thought that is triggering stress. If it is something that you have to worry about, schedule it to be worried about during the worry time. If it is something that needs to stop, command it to STOP. If it is something that needs to be buried, like regrets, mistakes, failures, animosity, or grudges, visualise that you are taking those thoughts deep underground and burying them sixty feet below the ground, never to resurface. This way, you can manage stress.

WORRY TIME TECHNIQUE

This is a strategy that involves setting aside a specific time each day to focus on thoughts that make you anxious instead of having anxious thoughts throughout the day and getting frequently stressed. This allows you to focus on thoughts that make you anxious and work out an action plan to ensure closure on that thought. For example, say you are worried about losing your job. During the worry time, you can focus on that thought that is making you anxious and work out a plan of action if you lose that job. If you have a plan in place, then that thought may not stress you.

SOCIAL CONNECTIONS

It helps manage stress, provides a buffer against stress, talks or discussions with family, friends, mentors, and coaches, helps redefine events to be less threatening, reduces anxiety, and gives a new perspective. The closer you are to people, the more warm the relationship feels as chemical oxytocin is released. Social connections reduce tension, reduce blood pressure, reduce stress hormones and increase feel-good hormones. Social Connection makes you more resilient and less reactive. It gives a sense of belonging and a secure sense of support. Practical solutions to the problems and challenges faced can come from social connections.

COOLING TECHNIQUE

This is a good way to manage stress. The technique is: when you feel stress is being triggered in your body, exhale deeply through your mouth, then inhale deeply through your nose. If you also utter the mantra "relax" when you breathe out and "calm" when you breathe in, it would add value.

YOUR KARMA TECHNIQUE

A young lady was quite hassled by her critical mother-in-law. The older woman from the old school of thought was critical of many things: the way the younger woman dressed, cooked, and maintained the house, and even if the young woman was delayed at work. This criticism was affecting her confidence, and her relationship with her husband started deteriorating. She decided to change her approach. Instead of getting angry, upset, or beating herself up when the senior lady criticised her, she said "Your Karma" within her mind and smiled. Karma means your actions now will lead to future consequences. The bad actions of the older lady will be punished by bad destiny. The young lady's reasoning was, why should I punish myself for her criticism? Her karma will get punished, and she refuses to get stressed. The older woman was bewildered by this changed approach, so she went to stay with her daughter.

TRUTH HAT TECHNIQUE

There is an interesting story about how Ms D'Souza saved her marriage. Her relationship with her husband was going through a rough patch. He was critical, unappreciative, and sulked. There were frequent arguments. He used to stay up late, and his alcohol consumption had increased. They decided to take a small holiday in Goa, and after they were more relaxed, one day, she surprised her husband with a hat and said, "We will play a little game. This hat is the **'Truth Hat'**. You wear this hat and tell me whatever the truth is, what is bothering you. I will listen and not be judgemental. Then I will wear the hat and tell you "the truth about what is bothering me, and you won't get judgemental." He did just that and shared what was bothering him. It was more about her not spending quality time with him. Then she wore the hat and told him the truth about him and what was bothering her. She agreed to mend her ways; he agreed to mend his ways. By sharing what was bothering them about their partner, it helped them reduce the causes of stress in their relationship. Even today, if one of the *partners is bothered by something, they wear the truth hat and communicate. The understanding is that the other partner will listen without getting upset, without getting prejudiced, and they can put up their point of view.*

A Stress Support Guide once employed the *Truth Hat Technique* to mend strained relationships within a dysfunctional family. The family consisted of two grown-up children who were constantly at odds with their parents, which led to heated arguments and emotional outbursts. Even minor criticism, observations or inconvenient suggestions often escalated into major flare-ups. Deep-seated prejudices had taken root, fostering misunderstanding and suspicions of hidden agendas.

The Stress Support Guide began by bringing all family members together and establishing clear ground rules. She explained that she would conduct one-on-one conversations with each family member to identify the sources of stress and behaviours or triggers that caused friction. This exercise would help uncover instances where someone's words or actions - often unintentional -might have been hurting others. Accumulated stress and unaddressed grievances, she explained, were fuelling the outbursts and disrupting harmony in the family.

However, she cautioned that the exercise required a mature and open mindset. It's natural for people to resist criticism, feel defensive or adopt a victim mindset, thinking,

"I am always blamed, I am always wronged and *other's are to be blamed"* For the exercise to succeed, each family member needed to listen to feedback without becoming emotional or resorting to self-blame. They had to view the process as an opportunity to clear misunderstandings, improve self-regulation, and rebuild trust.

Once the family agreed to these terms, the guide began her work. She met individually with each family member to understand their concerns and grievances. She then shared these insights with the relevant individuals, facilitating conversations to address specific issues. Through this iterative process, the family gradually became more aware of their own behaviours and the impact they had on others. Over time, this structured approach reduced misunderstandings, eased tensions and improved communication. The family learnt to manage their emotions better, paving the way for greater harmony and happiness. Thanks to the Stress Support Guide's patience and thoughtful use of the Truth Hat Technique, the once-dysfunctional family found a path towards healing and mutual understanding.

TOOLKIT TO MANAGE STRESS

Toolkit means some tools or useful equipment that are kept in a handy box ready to be used when needed. The tools that you can use to defuse stress include: 1) Reminding yourself to be human, 2) Changing thoughts that keep some thoughts that can instantly change your mood, 3) Cooling Technique, 4) Deep breathing technique, 5) Meditation Technique, 6) Mindfulness Technique, 7) Self-Talk, etc. The detailed techniques have been shared in other chapters; check the tactics that work for you. The toolbox here is your memory, and you have to use and recall the technique when stress is triggered. We need to appreciate that when our body is emotionally reacting, it is responding to save its life, and emotions like fear, anxiety, anger, upset, disappointments, etc., can be very strong. We need stronger stress-defusing techniques that can prevail over negative emotions. One of the strategies that is quite powerful is to use positive emotions to counter negative emotions. If you smile and laugh about the game that life is playing with you, you could trick the brain to trigger positive emotion or at least remain neutral.

MEDITATION TO MANAGE STRESS

There are many meditation techniques. One of the simplest is the mantra technique, wherein you repeat some words that are inconsequential or some calming words and chant them repeatedly. Meditation works because stress is triggered by negative thoughts, and thoughts are triggered automatically. If you engage your mind with some calming words that are repeated again and again, there can be no disturbing thoughts in your mind that can trigger stress, and you can feel calm. Try chanting calming words like 'calm' when you breathe in and 'relax' when you breathe out, or 'Om Shanthi' when you breathe in and 'Shanthi, Shanthi, Shanthi' when you breathe. Continuously chant for at least 5 minutes, not allowing any negative thoughts to disturb you, and experience the calmness and relaxation of your mind.

EXERCISE TO MANAGE STRESS

As exercise metabolises cortisol, the stress hormone, and increases endorphins, the feel-good hormones. Physical activity can distract you from stressful thoughts and worries, providing a mental break. Exercise triggers a relaxation response that counters the stress response. Exercise increases confidence and self-esteem. Exercise is a big help to manage stress. Do you have no time to exercise, meditate, do mindfulness, or do deep breathing exercises? There is no need to dedicate time to these exercises; you can do them at the office. Desk work can stress our back, neck, shoulders, etc. You can do stretching at regular intervals, which would help reduce stress on your body parts. You can walk up the stairs. You can walk during the lunch hour. Modern shopping centres and malls are also good places to walk if it is too warm outside. You can do meditation, mindfulness, and breathing exercises in the office; that would give the required rest to your mind and make you more productive.

QUICK STRESS CONTROL TIPS AT WORKPLACE

Some people want some tips on how to instantly control stress in the workplace.

- Talk could be a good stress control technique; you can internally tell yourself not to be an animal, to be human, to be in control, not to react, not to get emotional, etc.

- Reverse breathing could be a good technique. Deep breathing could be a good technique.

- Awareness of stress build up could be a good technique.

- Changing thought to distract. Visualisation of calm, serene, peaceful visual imagination helps.

- Bathroom Breaks, smiling, laughing, self-talk to let go, and forgiveness and forgetting are good techniques.

- Having positive vibes around your workspace, images of family and pets, images that remind you to be calm and serene, quotes and artefacts that act as a cue to help you remain calm help.

- Splashing water on the face, massaging the top of the head, and cupping and massaging the face also help.

PROBLEM-SOLVING TECHNIQUE

Underlying any stress response, there is a problem to which we are emotionally responding. But instead of emotions, if we respond rationally and use problem-solving techniques to solve the problem, it would help us manage our stress. The first step in problem-solving is to define the problem objectively and dispassionately without letting our ego and our emotions interfere. What is the problem? What is the root cause of the problem? Clearly understand the issue involved, be SRI, that is, be sensible and rational, and use your intelligence. Brainstorm solutions that is, work out possibilities and solutions, and evaluate the best possible option in the given situation. Sometimes consulting, doing research, and talking it out with family and friends also helps. Think of a person you admire and what he may have done if he were in the situation you are in. It also helps. Selecting the best possible solution, being persistent in implementing the solution, and doing the required course corrections help. If the problem is not addressed, the radar system within us will keep on reminding us about the problem; there will be repeated negative thoughts triggering stress.

COMPASSION TECHNIQUE

The pressure that you face could be from external sources that are not in your control. It may not be your fault and could be affecting you. The best support that you can give yourself is to be your friend. Treat yourself the way you would treat a friend who is facing challenges. Have a compassionate inner dialogue with yourself to make you feel calmer, relaxed, and more able to deal with stress. Avoid criticising or being harsh with yourself; you are already facing pressure, so don't add to it. Be aware of your feelings, reassure yourself, relax, take care of yourself, manage your emotions, and don't hurt yourself with fear, anxiety, anger, aggression, increased blood pressure, or pressure on your heart. Assure yourself that this too shall pass; these are all transient. Talk to yourself, motivate yourself, and be your own cheerleader.

POSITIVE SELF TALK TECHNIQUE

Our inbuilt radar system is constantly feeding us information in terms of thoughts, and most of the thoughts could be negative. Our minds have evolved to have constant thoughts, and we can't help it because that is how we are built. You can reduce the impact of negative mind chatter by intentionally and deliberately having positive self-talk with yourself. This helps counter negative thought patterns, regulate emotions, help reframe thoughts, boost confidence, reduce anxiety, enhance mood, and encourage problem-solving. You can set intentions, make affirmations, and talk to yourself as a coach, guide, or mentor. If you are going through a challenging time, regularly have positive self-talk with yourself, say at intervals of every hour. That would ensure that you are supported by a powerful person – yourself – and that would help you cope with all challenges.

GRATITUDE CAN HELP MANAGE STRESS

By practising gratitude, you are connected to powerful support that can help you cope with anything in life. Gratitude shifts your attention to the positive aspects of life, enhances positivity, and helps you sleep peacefully, knowing a powerful force is there to protect you. It increases resilience, making it easier to cope with life's challenges. Gratitude reduces negative emotions and increases acceptance. It is helpful to maintain a gratitude journal and express your gratitude every night before you retire; this practice will help you end the day with a positive frame of mind.

POSITIVITY JOURNAL

It is a journal that you keep where you maintain images of everything that makes you feel positive, happy, or laugh, giving you joy and triggering positive emotions. It could be an image of you posing with something that has brought happiness into your life, images of family, kids, happy moments, inspiring quotes, pictures of inspiring people, or notations of your thoughts. You can have some images that trigger positivity for you on your desk or wall so that there are positive vibes around you. Write a positive note to yourself and refer to that note whenever you need a little pick-me-up.

GROUNDING TECHNIQUES

These are strategies that help people reconnect with the present moment and distract them from negative thoughts or feelings. Some of the more popular grounding techniques are, **5, 4, 3, 2, 1** – that is, focus your awareness. Identify five things that you see in the room, four things you can touch, three things you can hear, two things you can smell, and one thing you can taste. This technique is useful to manage stress and anxiety.

BODY SCAN TECHNIQUE

In this technique, you mentally scan your body by directing your attention to a body part. Begin from the top of your head, where you may have tension headaches because of stress. Be aware of sensations of pain, tension, and discomfort. Breathe deeply, directing your breath to that body part. Visualise that body part expanding as the breath fills in there, then slowly release the breath. Visualise the body part on which you have your attention as deflating. You can then move to other body parts: your head, eyes, face, shoulders, back, stomach, legs, thighs, toes, etc. You can spend as much time as required to relax that body.

This technique can relax any body part where you can feel stress and tension. You can also focus your awareness on your anger, irritation, frustration, disappointment, fear, anxiety, etc. This technique is very useful to manage stress, anxiety, depression, etc.

STRESS BALL

It is a ball made of tactile material that can be squeezed and released. This action distracts attention and channelises energy towards the material object, thus reducing tension. Squeezing and releasing a stress ball creates an action of contraction and release of muscles, which contracts and releases tension, relaxing our muscles and relieving pain, headaches, etc. There have been some studies on the usage of stress balls, which have shown that the anxiety levels of some patients who were told to squeeze a stress ball before surgery had reduced. Even some students reported less anxiety about exams after they were asked to use a stress ball.

PROGRESSIVE MUSCLE TECHNIQUE

Involves tensing and relaxing muscle groups. Unlike the body scan technique, where you squeeze and release tense body parts by visualising expansion and contraction through breath, PMR allows you to physically relax your muscles. You start with your toes and progress upward.

In this technique, you start by lying or sitting down to relax your body. Lift your toes upwards, tense, and then relax. Move to the calves, tense, then relax; tense the thighs, relax, and repeat the process on the other leg. Tense your buttocks, relax, tense your stomach, relax, clench your hands, relax, contract your stomach, relax, tighten your chest, relax, raise your shoulders, relax, open your mouth wide, relax, close your eyes tightly, relax, lift your eyebrows, relax, smile widely, and relax. By physically contracting and then releasing, it helps relax the muscles and relieve stress.

STRESS BUSTERS

Stress is triggered by negative emotions. You can burst stress by deliberately generating positive emotions. Smiling and laughter are good stress busters because, for some reason, when you smile or laugh, the automatic negative thoughts cease to get triggered. Smiling and laughter also release feel-good hormones like endorphins, dopamine, etc., and make you feel good and happy, countering bad feelings like sadness, frustration, anxiety, etc. Sleep is an amazing stress buster. It metabolises cortisol, the stress hormone, reduces anxiety, lowers blood pressure, balances regular body functions, aids digestion, builds and repairs cells, flushes toxins, and gets you energised. Dancing also releases feel-good chemicals like endorphins and serotonin in the brain that make you feel calm, happy, and charged up. Dance reduces the stress hormone cortisol. People smile, laugh, and are happy when they dance. Dancing is also a form of exercise. It improves flexibility and suppleness and reduces anxiety and depression. It can be a creative outlet, giving a lot of satisfaction to the creative self and putting yourself in a positive frame of mind. Drawing, colouring, and painting can calm your brain. They engage your brain and senses in a creative pursuit, focusing your attention outside to an activity that does not provoke or agitate. Your mind is disengaged from disturbing thoughts. Drawing, colouring, painting, etc., are used in therapy for a hyperactive mind. Focusing on a creative outlet quiets the neurons from making connections. Art has been connected to flow, a state of deep engagement, if the person is engrossed in the activity. It is known to reduce stress. Singing and music are also great stress busters. They appeal to the pleasure centre of the brain, making you happy. Positive emotion reduces negative emotions. They improve mood, provide relaxation, lower anxiety, and reduce stress levels. Being active is a great stress buster. Focusing outside, keeping busy instead of wasting time on getting depressed, wallowing in self-pity, etc. Being connected, seeking support, sharing, and meeting friends are all great stress busters. Similarly, going for a picnic, watching a movie, reading an inspiring book, and following your hobby could be great stress busters. Cuddling is also a great stress buster because it releases feel-good hormones called oxytocin, which reduces the stress hormone cortisol and helps you calm down.

Exercise also reduces stress. It reduces stress hormones like cortisol, as well as calms down the rush of adrenaline. It relaxes muscles that have become tense due to stress.

FIVE MINUTES MEDITATION TECHNIQUES

You can meditate for just five minutes to destress, reduce tension, calm your mind, regain focus, be mindful of your thoughts, change your mood, and do deep breathing. A five-minute break after an hour of work could enhance your productivity. You don't need a special place or ambience; you can meditate at your office, in your home, whenever you feel restless or you find your mind jumping around, unable to focus. You can meditate to recharge a tired mind. You can meditate to create a gap between assignments; you can meditate to switch off.

Process of Five-Minute Meditation to Calm: Close your eyes and bring your awareness to your breath. Be aware of shallow breath, rapid breathing, and increased heartbeats. Deeply exhale, wait to the count of five, and then deeply inhale. While breathing out, say, *'Relax'*. Breath in saying *'Calm'*. Breathe out *'Relaxes'*. Breath in *'Calm'*. A variation could be that you visualise a calming bluish hue air being breathed in that has a calming effect and that air getting exhaled in pale pink, taking out all stress and tension.

Process of Five-Minute Meditation to Focus: Close your eyes and focus your awareness on your breath for some moments. As soon as you feel you are calming down, with your eyes closed, visualise big, bold work, such as 'FOCUS,' projected on the inner part of the forehead, and focus your attention on the word. You may find it hazy at the beginning, but maintain your focus. You may find the projection darkening but again getting hazy. Your monkey mind wants to jump around and detest being disciplined, made to focus, but the more you focus on **'FOCUS'**, the more you can discipline your mind.

Process of Five-Minute Mindfulness: Close your eyes, imagine yourself to be watching your mind from a tower, focus your awareness on your mind, observe, witness the thoughts floating in, don't get attached to the thought, don't react to the thought. You are just witnessing the thought, like clouds that appear in the sky, the thoughts will drift in, and poof, they would disappear, and then new thoughts will drift in. You are just being observant of thoughts coming in and drifting out. You are not reacting; you are being more in control, and you are not your thoughts. Thoughts are mental cognition, and you are mindful of it being just cognition. By being mindful, you are in control of your thoughts; your thoughts don't control you.

Process of Five-Minute Mood Changer: What triggers a bad mood or negative thoughts? You may not be aware of the thoughts; they could be there on your subconscious level, but negative thoughts manifest in the form of negative emotion, stress, bad mood, procrastination, depression, etc. How can you change your mood and your thoughts? Try this experiment. Close your eyes, think of everything that makes you happy: that baby, that kid, that song, that dance, that food, that celebration, happy, joyous occasion, that moment, that recognition, that reward, that accomplishment, open your eyes enjoy the happy and good mood, feel the charge, feel the sunshine within you. You may argue that if there is something negative going on, there are going to be negative thoughts; how do artificially changing thoughts and changing moods help?

PRESSURE POINT TECHNIQUES

Pressure points are parts of the body that can be massaged or pressed to reduce stress or tension. They are known as acupoints or meridian points in Chinese alternative medicine. The acupressure and acupuncture treatments are based on releasing stress at the pressure points. Pressure point meditation can be practised to release stress or tension; this practice involves massaging or putting slight pressure on pressure points, focusing our attention on the pressure points combined with deep exhalation and inhalation. This meditation combines acupressure, mindfulness, and breathing techniques. Our mind attains a meditative state as it is focused on pressure points and not indulging in automatic negative thinking. There are ten pressure points on your head and face, and you can release energy by gently massaging the pressure points for a minute. If you think that messes with your hair or find the massage more intense, then you can simply apply pressure that you are comfortable with. The Chinese have names for these pressure points, such as Yin-Tang, Tai-Yang, San-Jio, Feng-Chi, Feng Fu, Tianzhu, etc. We are just describing the area where the pressure point is located in English. Gently massage or press the pressure point for relief from stress and tension.

- Pressure Point 1: Crown, the topmost part of our head.

- Pressure Point 2: Frontal – the front part of your head.

- Pressure Point 3: Third Eye: The centre between the two eyebrows above the nose bridge.

- Pressure Point 4: Forehead: The centre of the forehead.

- Pressure Point 5: Eyes: Gently touch or massage your eyes to release tension.

- Pressure Point 6: Temporal: a depression area at the side of your face in line with eyebrows.

- Pressure Point 7: Pressure point before the ears, when massaged, gives relief from headache.

- Point 8: Medulla: These are slight mounds at the back of the head. Just gently touch this area because the nerves that supply blood to your brain meet here. Do not apply pressure or massage this area. Please don't touch it if you don't feel comfortable.

- Pressure Point 9: Face: There are many pressure points in the face. Gently massaging the face gives relief against stress and tension.

- Pressure Point 10: Palm of the hand: The palm contains many pressure points. Rubbing the palms together relieves stress and tension.

MINDFULNESS TECHNIQUES

Mindfulness is the ability to be fully present in the moment, aware of what is happening in your body, watching that as a witness, and not being affected by that. You are like the higher person, being aware of the thoughts, sensations, and moments that you are in, being detached, non-reactional, non-judgemental, just being aware. Your attention is not in the past nor anxious about the future; you are present, and you are present in the now. You can be mindful of many things.

Mindful Thinking: When you close your eyes, be aware of thoughts that are floating into your mind. You are not reacting to them, being judgemental, feeling anxiety, fear, or upset about them; you are just **unattached and still** aware of the thoughts that are being triggered automatically. By being aware and focusing your attention on your thoughts, the number of thoughts getting triggered reduces, and they also lose their potency.

Mindful Breathing: You can be mindful of your breath, inhale slowly, visualise how the cool blue air is travelling to your head, clearing all blocks, travelling to your lungs, cleaning and clearing all blocks on the way, and then after cleaning and clearing exits all toxins from your body in the form of exhalation, even 10 minutes of mindful breathing may make you feel fresh, clean, and clear.

Mindful Eating: Pay attention to what you eat or pick up any fruit to eat; pay attention to the colour, shape, texture, and aroma. Pay attention to your bite; when your teeth plunge into the fruit, pay attention to juice spurting, the distinct taste of the juice and the fruit, the taste evolving when you slowly eat the fruit. Chew it slowly with awareness, if not thirty-two times, then at least fifteen times. Be in gratitude for the fruit, relish, and enjoy.

Mindful Walking: Pay attention to each step, be aware of the sensation, if possible, walk barefoot on the grass, and feel how the grass feels underneath your feet. Your focus and attention should be on each step, the sensation when you raise your feet, when you land your feet on the ground, and the pressure on your feet when you land; focus on minute details. When your attention is totally immersed, you will be in a state of flow.

Mindful Of Your Senses: Be aware and focus your attention on five things you can see. Focus on the thing you are seeing for at least a minute. Now, be aware of four things you can hear; focus on the thing that you hear. Pay attention to your heartbeat, the beat in your brain, and the sounds in the room or outside. Notice that when you become conscious, when your attention is outside your mind, your mind does not have negative thoughts. Maintain your focus for at least a minute on each thing you hear. Now, be aware of your touch, the sensory nerves in your palm, the relaxing feel of a massage on the top of your head, and the relaxation of your eyes by a soft sensory rub. Do this for at least a minute. Notice how it relaxes you. Now, focus your awareness on two things that you can smell. Maybe you feel that you don't smell anything, but because you have not been mindful, you are not aware of the smells. Once you focus your awareness, you will notice many smells that you are exposed to. Just focus on two of the smells for a minute. You can also be mindful of how your head feels by focusing on any heaviness in your mind. When you are mindful, you are not thinking; you become detached from thoughts, you are not stressed, and you are in a meditative state, a state of flow.

SLEEP TECHNIQUE

Sleep is the body's natural stress buster. Rest and relaxation reduce stress. The body repairs and restores itself when you sleep. Sleep can increase your mental function, concentration, and creativity, reduce your tiredness and fatigue, improve decision-making, and make you feel better, happy, and relaxed. However, many people are finding it increasingly difficult to sleep. Why? The reason is if you are stressed, it becomes difficult to sleep. As we said earlier, a simple way to understand stress is that it is an urge in your body to fight or run. Why? Because you are feeling threatened, there could be uncertainty, insecurity, anger, upset, frustration, fear, anxiety, disappointment, etc. The watchman in your brain would be hyper-aroused; it could be triggering all kinds of negative thoughts in your mind. Understand from the perspective of your brain, the message it is getting from your negative thoughts is that you are under attack; your brain wants to protect. It will not let you sleep so that you are ready to fight or run. You know, and I know, that we humans don't face the same threat that our ancestors, the early humans, faced. The negative thoughts that are being triggered are a warning or alert about some problem or challenges. These are not going to kill us; there is no reason to lose sleep over it. But in automatic mode, it is the duty of our survival brain to keep on reminding us and keep us awake, so there could be constant negative thoughts that could be keeping us awake. What can we do about it?

Settle your worries much before sleeping: The Buddhist monk has a term for our mind; it is called monkey mind or your monkey inside you. Why? Because it keeps on jumping here and there, it can keep you in a state of arousal. What can you do about it? Try Thought Management. What is Thought Management? It is estimated that at the subconscious or non-conscious level, we may have sixty thousand thoughts in a day. Threats to our well-being like losing our job, facing setbacks, going broke, divorce, death, or falling seriously ill are not something that keeps on happening, but the challenge that we face is that our survival mind would be nervous, anxious, keep on having automatic thoughts, etc. There is a need to have confidence in oneself; don't cross the bridge until you come to it. Problems are temporary, and they always pass. More than 90% of the time, we are having recurring thoughts and useless thoughts and getting anxious about the same thing again and again. What is the maximum that can happen? We are not going to lose our lives, and there are nearly eight billion people in the world who have one hundred billion requirements; we obviously are good enough to take care of ourselves and our families. So don't worry.

If you are not able to stop your worries, **hand it to God**. You have taken care of your worries all day; now it is time to sleep. Your body and mind need rest and relaxation. You need to be recharged; you can't keep on worrying night and day. So, if you are not able to stop worries, hand it over to whichever God you believe in. God does not need to sleep; it is your friend with whom you can share your fear, anxiety, uncertainty, insecurities, etc. If you can't express yourself, write a note to God, maintain a journal, and sleep peacefully. If negative thoughts get triggered, firmly command your monkey mind to stop jumping around and getting worried. God is in charge while you are sleeping; instruct the monkey in you not to disturb you; the heaven will not fall while you are sleeping.

Expressing gratitude for positive things in life improves sleep: There is a state that feeling grateful helps people sleep better and longer. That is because thankfulness for positive things before you sleep reduces negative thoughts. Maintain a gratitude diary or just sleep; ask yourself, "What am I grateful for today?" Keep on asking the question. Keep on being thankful for everything that has been showered in your life by the benevolence of the higher power; the negative thoughts and negativity will dissipate, and you will have peace and serenity descending on you. Sleep peacefully.

Digitally disconnect at least an hour before you go to bed: Disconnect from work, email, messaging service, and social media; disconnect from anything that can get you worked up. Disconnect from the blue light emission from digital devices that confuses your brain and interferes with circadian rhythm. It not only allows you to rest and relax but also allows your mind to rest and relax; it lets the brain release melatonin, the sleep hormone that drifts you to a peaceful sleep.

Warm Bath, Warm Cup of Milk, A Relaxing Book helps you drift to sleep. Your body and mind need to rest and relax. A warm bath would wash away the fatigue and tiredness of the day and relax your muscles; a warm cup of milk may help you to sleep as milk contains sleep-promoting nutrients like tryptophan, magnesium, and melatonin, this may give you a feeling of peace and relaxation. A relaxing book can reduce mind chatter, distract, create a greater sense of calm and relaxation, and help you sleep. Sleep is a process; it is difficult to immediately fall asleep as soon as you put your head on the pillow; the chatter in the mind and the thoughts that stimulate are to be reduced; this is a gradual process.

YOGA NIDRA TECHNIQUE

Yoga Nidra is a meditation/mindfulness practice that is done lying down. It has been found useful to reduce stress, anxiety, and insomnia in many controlled studies. It has been found to reduce blood pressure and heart rate, induce rest and relaxation, and allow access to delta brain waves, which accelerate healing and relaxation during deep sleep. Yog Nidra activates the parasympathetic nervous system, which reduces the activity of the sympathetic nervous system, which is responsible for triggering stress in our body.

It is a very simple technique where you lie down in a relaxed state. Be mindful of the breath being inhaled and exhaled; let your breath relax; be mindful of your heart; let your heart relax; be mindful of your brain; let the brain relax; be mindful of your thoughts; relax, relax, relax. Now, take your awareness to your small left toe, relax all your toes in your left foot, and relax your ankle, calves, and thighs. Relax your small toe on your right foot, relax, relax all the toe fingers, relax, ankle, calves, thighs, relax all body parts in your legs, then move your awareness to other body parts, relax, relax, relax, let go, sleep, don't resist, relax. You can do Yoga Nidra with many guided meditations available online. Yoga Nidra can help you destress and give you a heavenly, relaxed feeling.

JOURNALING TECHNIQUE

Journaling is a good technique to manage stress. Writing down your thoughts helps you process them. When you are writing, your eyes, your hand, and your brain are engaged, which helps you disengage disturbing thoughts that may be running through your mind. By writing in your journal, or as some prefer to call it, a diary, you provide a safe outlet to express your emotions. Writing helps you organise your thoughts and make sense of complex emotions, leading to better self-understanding. Writing enables problem-solving; by exploring stressors on paper, you can brainstorm solutions, leading to an action plan that can reduce feelings of helplessness. Journaling also helps you identify thought patterns and responses that can assist in addressing recurring issues. Writing reduces rumination as you are not dwelling on the same thing repeatedly. Through writing, you eliminate confusion and preoccupation, becoming more aware and clearer about your thoughts and feelings. You create a sense of control that aids in managing stress.

CHAPTER 9
STORIES ON HANDLING STRESS

These stories are inspired by real events. Names, characters, places and incidents have been changed at the request of those involved to protect their privacy. Any resemblance to actual persons, living or deceased, or to real events, places, or organisations is purely coincidental. The intent is to offer a narrative that respects privacy while conveying themes inspired by true experiences.

JAY BHANUSHALI

Jay, a young lawyer on the brink of burnout, had been working over 16 hours daily, with weekends consumed by urgent merger and acquisition deals. The high-pressure assignment, vital for a client's IPO launch during a bullish market, left him mentally exhausted and slipping in his work. One misstep - missing confirmation details from creditors - delayed the acquisition and brought him harsh feedback from his firm's principal partner. Jay was demoralised and ready to quit the profession altogether until a family member suggested he speak with SSG, a Stress Support Guide group specialising in stress management techniques. The SSG offered Jay a roadmap with actionable suggestions.

Suggestion 1: Express Emotions

The guides encouraged Jay to talk with a confidant, whether a friend or a family member, to lighten his burden. If that wasn't possible, he could pour his thoughts into a journal. By venting, he could clear some of the mental fog that had taken over.

Suggestion 2: Take Micro-Breaks and Practice Mindfulness

Jay was told to take five-minute breaks each hour to reset his mind and body. These "micro-breaks" involved deep breathing exercises to boost oxygen levels and refresh his brain. Simple meditation techniques, like mantra repetition and mindfulness techniques, like grounding 5-4-3-2-1, were also recommended. Stretching his body at regular intervals with emphasis on the neck, back and shoulders was recommended to reduce stress in the body. A quick walk or power nap in the afternoon would help him perk up and metabolise cortisol, the stress hormone. These practices would keep his physical and mental energy up, even during gruelling days.

Suggestion 3: Learn to Say "No" and establish Boundaries and Delegate

One of the most challenging yet essential strategies was setting boundaries. Jay needed to communicate when he was overloaded and clarify the priority of tasks with his seniors. The guides urged him to delegate more, letting junior associates handle research and routine tasks, which he could check at scheduled intervals for progress.

Suggestion 4: Use Time Wisely and Limit Distractions

SSG suggested Jay track his time by maintaining a worksheet to see where he was losing hours. He realised that waiting for instructions and attending unnecessary meetings ate up significant time. To combat interruptions, he started marking his cubicle with a "Do Not Disturb" sign during deep work sessions, allowing colleagues to contact him via message or email instead. Jay also scheduled specific time slots to respond to emails and messages to avoid distractions.

Suggestion 5: Prioritise Rest

Jay was advised to leave the office at set time, get 7-8 hours of sleep, and resist the urge to stay late to impress the partners. With enough sleep, he found he could think more clearly and work more effectively. To his surprise, his firm's partners soon noticed his improved productivity and efficiency, even with lesser hour spent in the office. They began discussing the possibility of making him a junior partner to ensure he stayed with the firm.

Suggestion 6: Separate Work from Personal Life

SSG emphasised the importance of leaving work-related stress at the office.

Jay learnt to compartmentalise, making a mental separation between his work and home life. He also began spending weekends on hobbies, meeting friends and unwinding. Volunteering for a programme teaching the underprivileged youth gave him a new sense of purpose and fulfilment. Jay not only mastered his workload but regained his passion for law. He became more resilient, balanced and successful lawyer realising that handling stress well was the key to both his professional and personal happiness.

SID KULKARNI

Sid had spent over 20 years working diligently in the information technology sector, climbing his way to a mid-managerial position in IT support for a large American retail company. However, as the retail landscape shifted due to online competitors like Amazon and Alibaba, the company began to struggle. The pandemic proved too much for its already fragile state, and after a period of extended store closures, the company filed for bankruptcy. It was bought by a hedge fund solely interested in real estate, leading to the closure of over a thousand stores and mass layoffs - including Sid.

The timing couldn't have been worse. Sid had used much of his savings during the pandemic, and though he had spent time upgrading his skills, he found that his expertise was now outdated. The job market had moved on to new demands like Artificial Intelligence, and Sid, now in his mid-forties, found himself competing with younger, more technically adept and lower-cost candidates. Rejections piled up, each one deepening his frustration and eroding his self-worth. Coming from a background where joblessness was stigmatised. Sid was too ashamed to tell his family. Each morning, he would leave the house as if going to work, only to spend hours wandering the city or at cyber cafes, applying for positions that seemed further and further out of reach.

As weeks went by, anxiety and despair crept in. Sid's mind became a storm of negative thoughts, clouded by fear and anger. His sleep suffered, his blood pressure soared, and his physical health began to deteriorate. It was his father who, sensing the hidden struggle, suggested that Sid meet with a Stress Support Guide (SSG), an organisation that connects people with wise mentors to offer support in times of crisis. Reluctantly, Sid agreed to meet a Senior Guide, a retired school principal whose calm wisdom slowly encouraged Sid to open up. The Guide offered Sid five simple yet profound suggestions.

1. Embrace Truth Over Hiding

The Guide urged Sid to tell his family the truth about his job loss. Hiding his situation was only creating more stress, he explained. Honesty would allow Sid to free himself from the constant need to pretend, which was draining his energy and self-respect. By being open, Sid could also allow his loved ones to support him, lessening his burden.

2. Accept, Don't Resist

Instead of battling with his situation, Sid was encouraged to accept it. Fighting against reality was exhausting his mental and physical resources. By accepting the situation, Sid could think clearly and begin to see new possibilities rather than by being paralysed by resistance.

3. Prioritise Physical Health

Physical exercise was next on the list. Sid learnt that regular activity would release endorphins to boost his mood, along with dopamine, a natural reward hormone. Exercise would also metabolise cortisol, a stress hormone, and improve his resilience in facing challenges. The Guide advised Sid to get sunlight exposure daily to lift his spirits and support vitamin D production, which is crucial for mental well-being.

4. Structure the Day

Sid found it challenging to stay motivated without a job. The Guide suggested a structured routine, setting specific times for sleep, exercise, networking, relaxation. To combat sleeplessness, Sid was encouraged to disconnect from screens an hour before bed and practice calming techniques like Yog Nidra, (PMR) progressive muscle relaxation.

5. Discover His Ikigai

Perhaps the most transformative suggestion was for Sid to reflect on his **Ikigai** -the Japanese concept of finding one's purpose. He was to find his passion, which would give him his mission; he could have a vision, and it could become his profession. He was to identify what he would enjoy doing, that he is good at, what he would be doing is required, and people would be happy to pay the price for that. Through these exercises, Sid discovered that he had a passion for teaching maths and physics, subjects he had always enjoyed. Demand for private tutoring was high, particularly among students in international programmes who could pay well. Sid found joy and fulfilment in teaching and was soon recognised for his skills.

As Sid's reputation grew, he began to attract students through word of mouth, even taking on consulting work with a startup building an educational app. His income surpassed what he'd earned at his corporate job without the relentless pressure. Now, Sid is able to balance tutoring, consulting and personal time, building a life of both purpose and stability. Sid's journey of resilience didn't just help him rebuild his life; it inspired him to give back to society. Today, he also serves as a Guide with SSG for others facing similar challenges, finding fulfilment in helping others find their own paths.

PARESH MISHRA

Paresh grew up in a small, close-knit town where dreams of stardom were seldom encouraged, yet his passion for acting was undeniable. When he secured a spot at the prestigious National School of Drama in Delhi, it was nothing short of a miracle. His family, though sceptical, believed in his potential. They borrowed heavily to fund his education, hoping that one day he would achieve greatness and repay their faith. But Delhi's theatre world was competitive, and despite his talent, Paresh found himself struggling to find work after graduation.

For nearly a year, he went without a break; the calls he had hoped for never came. The auditions that he had aced led to nowhere. His family's faith began to waver, and the pressure to send money back home became intense.

His parents needed help with their loan repayments, and they weren't shy about reminding him of it. Paresh began to feel the weight of their expectations, and his sleepless nights and anxious days became routine. He lost weight and constantly worried about his future and the family that was counting on him.

Then, a small flicker of hope arrived in the form of an art film director who offered him a character role. The director promised exposure but could only pay when the film found funds. Desperate, Paresh accepted, believing that any experience was better than none. But as months passed, he continued to struggle with rent and food, his 'parents' calls urging him to send money, and the endless anxiety about whether he'd ever make it.

During this dark period, Paresh met a guide from the Stress Support Guides (SSG). This guide saw his desperation and, in a calm yet practical manner, outlined a path to help him manage his stress and regain control. First, he recommended that Paresh "de-risk" by finding a job that could offer immediate payment. It didn't have to be acting; he just needed something steady to ease his financial worries. He also advised Paresh to create a support system, a group of people he could lean on. Exercise, meditation, journaling and mindfulness became his new allies, tools to quiet the storm in his mind. The guide also urged him to communicate openly with his parents about how their pressure was affecting him, and set boundaries with them in a respectful way.

With a structured schedule, Paresh began making small yet meaningful changes. He started networking more, managing his social media and strategically increasing his visibility in the film business. Over time, these efforts helped him build resilience; he felt a sense of purpose return. One day, while talking to a member of his support group, he heard that a major OTT platform was casting for a new web series with a regional theme - one that resonated deeply with his own background. The series was centred around gang rivalries in small towns, and for the first season, they needed actors who understood the local culture. Without hesitation, Paresh auditioned, and to his surprise and relief, he was selected immediately. The platform offered pre-episode payments, and for the first time, money started flowing in. His portrayal of a crafty, ambitious young man from a small town was met with widespread acclaim, and his fan base quickly grew.

Buoyed by this newfound success and confidence, Paresh approached the director of the art film, explaining that he could no longer work for free. He firmly requested payment for his past work, stating that he would have to stop if they couldn't compensate him. Although he faced threats and pushback, he didn't yield. The film was already six months in the making, and it was nearly impossible to replace him at that stage. In the end, the producers relented, settling his dues and even offering an advance. Today, Paresh Mishra is one of the top stars in OTT space. He is known for his authentic portrayals and commands a substantial fee for each project. His family has repaid all their debts and they are respected as one of the wealthiest families in their village. Paresh's journey from desperation to success is a testament to resilience, the power of support system and the life changing impact of managing stress.

REBECCA VAZ

Rebecca Vaz had always been driven, resilient and determined to make something of herself. Yet when she failed her final Chartered Accountancy exam, it shattered her. After investing years of hard work, countless sleepless nights, and almost all her energy into her studies, this setback felt like end of her dreams. Overwhelmed and deeply upset, Rebecca found herself standing at the door of Stress Support Guides (SSG) barely holding back her tears and contemplating abandoning her studies altogether. Her Guide greeted her warmly, his reassuring presence offering her much needed anchor. He listened patiently as she poured out her disappointment, and then with a calm smile, he reminded her that success and failure are just two sides of life. The spoke of setbacks as moments that help us learn and grow, rather than define us. *In the vast expanse of life, he said, this is just a blink"* You are not failing; you're learning. With this newfound perspective, Rebecca decided to give herself a second chance, re-registering for the exam. Her Guide suggested she analyse her previous mistakes, improve her study strategies and dedicate more time to revision and practice.

As they continued their sessions, her Guide noticed she always seemed stressed. He asked her to keep a "Stress Book," a personal journal to capture the thoughts triggering her stress. This simple act of writing her thoughts down helped her recognise underlying patterns. The Guide taught her that instead of reacting emotionally, she could respond with a *"sensible, rational, intelligent"* approach. One day, she shared something even more personal: Her constant battle with inner critic. The inner voice would endlessly criticise her and pull her into cycles of negative thinking. The Guide reassured her, explaining that everyone has an inner critic, but we don't have to let it control us. He encouraged her to practice mindfulness to challenge her negative thoughts, and to replace them with positive affirmations. He suggested techniques from Cognitive Behavioural Therapy (CBT) to reframe her negative thoughts. But the healing went even deeper, Rebecca finally revealed long held pain, her anger towards her father, who had left her and her mother to fend for themselves. She had buried years of hurt and resentment, and the Guide gently explained that holding onto this anger was like carrying a burning coal. He asked her to consider forgiving her father, not for his sake but for her own peace. And with great courage, Rebecca took the difficult step of contacting her father.

The conversation was emotional; both father and daughter broke down in tears. Rebecca learnt of his regrets and the pride he had always felt for her from afar, his ego having kept him from reaching out. This conversation marked the beginning of a new chapter. They met, shared their stories, and started building a fragile but growing bond. With time, she saw her family starting to heal. With her newfound sense of peace, Rebecca dove back into her studies with renewed focus and strength. This time she passed her Chartered Accountancy exams with high marks. She had not only achieved a great academic milestone but had found within herself a profound strength and wisdom. Today Rebecca stands on the brink of a promising career. Her journey taught her that life's setbacks are stepping stones, not stumbling blocks, and that embracing oneself with compassion can heal even the deepest wounds.

KEERAT KAUR

Keerat Kaur's life was defined by love, sacrifice, and resilience. But when the news arrived that her son, her only child, had fallen in combat, her world unravelled. Just a year before, her son had donned his Army uniform with pride, taking an oath to serve the nation. At that moment, Keerat felt like all her sacrifices had been worthwhile. But now, in the silence of his absence, it all felt unbearably empty. The loss compounded her grief over her husband, who had passed after a long fight with cancer. Now, with both gone, she felt adrift and alone.

Moving back to her parent's home in the city, far from the familiar surroundings of the cantonment, she became isolated from the Army's community support, making it difficult to access counselling. The weight of her grief was slowly turning into depression, a heavy cloud shadowed her every thought. Just as her hope was slipping away, she met Anna D'sa, a Stress Support Guide, with a warm smile and a compassionate presence. Recognising Keerat's pain, Anna gently encouraged her to meet a therapist. "Depression is like a dark fog, Keerat," Anna explained. "But you don't have to face it alone. Together, we can find a way through." They began taking long walks together, and during these moments, Keerat opened up, speaking her heart and slowly beginning to heal.

One day, Anna took her to a dog adoption meet-up, a community effort to find homes for stray animals. A small, skinny puppy with big, hopeful eyes caught her attention. When Keerat looked into the puppy's gaze, she saw a flicker of life and resilience - a mirror of her own heart. In that instant, she decided to adopt the puppy, Zorawar, who she named "brave" in memory of her son. Caring for Zorawar brought a sense of purpose and joy into her days, easing the heaviness of her grief. Anna continued to introduce Keerat to new experiences, including guiding sessions for underprivileged women. Listening to their stories of hardship and resilience stirred something in her; she felt a renewed sense of gratitude for the Army's support. At Anna's suggestion, she started a gratitude journal, recording five things each day for which she was thankful. Slowly, this practice brought light to her life, shifting her focus to the small moments of grace amidst the pain.

Recognising the need for meaningful engagement, Anna encouraged Keerat to join a group of Army Officers' wives who helped soldiers' widows navigate financial and educational concerns. Her natural empathy and strength made her a pillar of support for others, and soon, her healing journey became a beacon of hope for others. On her initiative, the group connected with a businesswoman who was running a microfinance venture. Inspired by Keerat's dedication, they started a self-help group, providing soldiers widows with advanced sewing machines to help them gain financial independence. In collaboration with a textile manufacturer, they created a line of unique garments that were sold across the country, generating both income and pride for the women.

Keerat's efforts didn't go unnoticed. The government awarded her for her contributions to women's welfare, but for her, the true reward was seeing the hope and resilience return to the eyes of the women she had helped. Her grief had been her path to service. And her pain transformed into purpose. Through her journey, Keerat learnt that resilience does not mean an absence of pain but rather the courage to keep moving forward and to find purpose even in the darkest of moments. With Zorawar by her side and a new mission in her heart, she embraced life once more - not just for herself but for those who counted on her strength. In healing others, she had healed herself, proving that even from the greatest losses, a life of love and purpose could emerge.

PRIYA SHAH

Priya found herself standing at a crossroads in life, facing a mountain of challenges. A year into what should have been a new chapter of love and companionship, Priya had come back to her parental home. Her marriage had been anything but happy; her husband, addicted to drugs, had treated her terribly after enduring a painful cycle of neglect and abuse. Priya finally found the courage to leave.

Returning home, however, was not the comfort Priya had hoped it would be. Her mother was disappointed and often subtly hinted that Priya should have stayed in marriage. With her younger sister's marriage still to be arranged, her mother worried that Priya's divorce might cast a shadow over the family's social standing.

These unspoken expectations weighed heavily on Priya. The emotional toll manifested in different ways: sleepless nights, constant anxiety and soon unhealthy habits. She started overeating to fill the emotional void and went on shopping sprees, filling up her closet with clothes and accessories she hardly needed. Her aggression and irritability grew, leading to arguments and misunderstandings with those around her. One evening, exhausted by her own restlessness, Priya called up a friend, who in the recent past seemed to have become very calm and composed. Her friend talked about a new group that she had joined, which was helping her manage her stress. At her friend's invitation, she attended one of the sessions of Stress Support Guides. Here, she met others who, like her, were navigating life's twists and turns. The group was guided by a calm and empathetic man who listened to Priya's story without judgement. The guide encouraged Priya to look beyond temporary relief and explore ways to truly manage her emotions and rebuild her sense of self.

The support group became a safe haven with the guide guidance. Priya learnt to channel her emotions constructively. Instead of reaching for snacks or impulsively shopping, she discovered the benefits of exercise, yoga, and meditation. Slowly, she also began to develop a healthy relationship with food, following a balanced diet that nourished both her body and mind. Yoga and meditation helped her find inner peace, and over time, she noticed a profound change within herself. She felt lighter, not just physically but also emotionally, and her mind became clearer and her spirit calmer.

With her newfound confidence, Priya transformed. She was no longer the anxious, withdrawn woman she once had been. Instead, she was becoming vibrant, poised and radiant. People began to notice the positive shift in her demeanour, especially at her workplace. One of her colleagues was a kind-hearted young man who had been observing Priya's journey from a distance. Her courage and resilience captured his attention and respect, and he admired her quiet strength.

One evening, as Priya was leaving work, he mustered up the courage to approach her. He expressed his admiration for her strength, and what had begun as a conversation about resilience soon turned into something much more meaningful. He confessed his feelings and hoped she'd consider taking a chance on love again. Priya felt a sense of gratitude not just for his words but for the path she had walked to get there. She realised she was no longer the same person, and her heart, once burdened by pain and anxiety, was now open to new possibilities. Her journey had taught her resilience and self-love, and she was ready to embrace a life shaped by her own choices.

CHAPTER 10
TAKE UP THE CHALLENGE

"Being challenged in life is inevitable; being defeated is optional,"

– Roger Crawford

Taking on challenges is often seen as stressful, but paradoxically, it can be a powerful way to reduce stress and achieve success. Facing challenges head-on enables growth, builds resilience, and transforms adversity into opportunity. Many successful individuals started with failures or setbacks but achieved greatness because they embraced challenges rather than avoiding them.

TAKING UP THE CHALLENGE REDUCES STRESS

When faced with challenges, we often perceive stress as negative. But stress can serve as an alarm; stress can caution, and it could serve as a warning that something is bothering our mind. It would be negative if stress controls us, but it may be great positive if we control stress and use it to our advantage. Understand how, when there is a negative situation, our brain may perceive the situation to be a threat to our life and activate our body to fight or run to save its life. But we know most of the negative situations in the life of modern humans could be temporary problems and challenges in life. They are not physical threats to life, but there could be risks to quality of life. The solution is not in getting stressed, fighting or running like an animal, but the solutions may be in feeling challenged and using the drive, intelligence, patience and perseverance to work out long-term solutions.

How not to feel stressed but to feel challenged? The method is not to feel bad, have fear, get anxious, get angry or upset about the problem you are facing, the reason being our brain triggers stress when it figures out that we do not like the situation and are having negative emotions and feeling about the same, but if we don't have negative feeling but feel challenged, there is pressure to meet the challenge, but we are not getting threatened by the situation, there is no fear, anger, there is no tension, no negative emotion, no negative feelings but call to rise up and meeting the challenge, there is positive stress that ignites inner drive and passion. Instead of worrying about the problem, the focus moves to solving it. Challenges activate adrenaline and other stress hormones that, when harnessed, boost energy, focus and performance.

There is a sense of purpose; taking on the challenge gives life meaning, reducing the stress of aimlessness. Take the case of Dhirubhai Ambani, when the Yemenis threw British businesses and people working for them out of Aden in an armed struggle. Dhirubhai was in bad shape; his family was young, Mukesh Ambani was just one year of age, they had given up their house and all assets, his father had just been a poor Government School teacher in Chorwad, he was in no position to support Dhirubhai who had gone to Aden to escape poverty, coming to Mumbai with just about thousands pound, worth just fifteen thousand rupees those days, residing in a rented tenement in Bhuleshwar, sharing rented premises in Narshi Natha Street Kalbadevi, not knowing what is going to trade, suffering losses in many initial trading businesses they set up. His cousin and partner left the partnership because he could not figure out how Dhirubhai was going to succeed, so he quit the partnership, but Dhirubhai was unfazed; he had taken up the challenge to succeed, and he would find a way to succeed no matter what.

Challenges build confidence and resilience: - When you take up the challenge, there is inner drive, passion, grit and determination. It becomes a matter of honour to succeed. There is confidence that you will find a way out and eventually succeed even if the situation is difficult. Failures become stepping stones, teaching valuable lessons and toughening mental strength.

Challenges encourage personal growth and skill development: Challenges push individuals out of their comfort zone, forcing them to learn, adapt, and grow. To overcome obstacles, people often acquire new knowledge or develop unique strategies. Challenges teach flexibility, an essential skill for handling stress and uncertainty. Gautam Adani did his B'com, but working as an Accounts clerk would not have made his money, so he learnt diamond trading and did brokerages for Mahendra Brothers at Opera house, standing in the lane behind Panchratna Building and having innumerable cutting chai. A call from his elder brother to manage their plastic unit in Ahmedabad, where their family savings had been locked, made him go to Ahmedabad, where he soon realised that being a scale manufacturer was not going to help him survive; the money was in importing raw material, and he soon learnt the tricks of the trade to import PVC which earned him big profits enabling him to start trading in a big way.

Challenges cultivate patience, perseverance, determination, creativity and innovation: - Taking up challenges requires and reinforces traits like patience and perseverance, which are crucial for success. Take the case of Nitin and Nikhil Kamat of Zerodha, who belong to the GSB community in the South Kanara district of Karnataka and believe in high education and secure employment in the Bank. Their father was working at Canara Bank, but these brothers developed an interest in stock investment, which was considered gambling by that community. These brothers dropped out of college and worked in call centres at night, answering phone calls. In the daytime, they shared investing from the meagre amount of salary they earned. They were looked down upon in their community, which believed in high education and white-collar jobs where doing business was considered to be risky. Slowly, they started to invest for other people and got some good returns; they soon realised that if they had to grow, they would have to invest in technology, so they, along with a techie, developed software which enabled online investment. They soon realised that online, whether a person invests a thousand rupees or a million rupees, the time and process remained the same, so instead of charging a percentage, they charged a small amount for trade, irrespective of the amount involved. They also made the process of opening a Demat account very easy and offered a free opening for Demat account openings. Business exploded; they became the largest brokerage in India handling more than one hundred-billion-dollar trade in the National Stock Exchange. They are making profits in excess of 2000 crores (300 million dollars). They were embarrassed to pay Rs 100 crore (14 million dollars) in salary per year, sheepishly explaining that they had to take a salary as most of the profit was being paid as taxes. They have refused investments in their company and made a big pile for themselves; as Nitin, the elder brother, explains, we don't want money, and we don't know what we are going to do with it. What makes them happy is the fact that they took up the challenges that proved that even a middle-class person has the right to dream. They invest in big ways in start-ups, support others to succeed, and inspire others by sharing their stories and insights.

Taking up challenges is not only a pathway to reducing stress but also a catalyst for personal and professional success by confronting obstacles. Taking up the challenges transforms stress into a source of energy and focus. Build resilience and confidence to handle adversity and unlock creativity and innovation, leading to unique solutions. It cultivates patience, perseverance, and determination; it becomes a source of deep satisfaction and a sense of achievement and fulfilment from overcoming difficulties.

1. SACHIN TENDULKAR

Sachin Tendulkar, the legendary Indian batsman, has etched his name among the world's greatest cricketers, but the world may not have had Sachin Tendulkar if he had not taken one decision quite early in his career, that is to take on the challenge. The story is that Sachin had impressed the Indian Cricketing Board in School Cricket, and at the age of 16, he was selected to represent India in the Test Series against Pakistan. Sachin made his debut when the Pakistani pace bowler trinity of Imran Khan, Wasim Akram, and Waqar

Younis were at their fearsome best. In the fourth test at Sialkot, India was down with four wickets and just 36 runs. Most of the top-order batsmen had lost their wickets, and Pakistani pace bowlers were all charged up. Sachin was sent to bat; he was not wearing a grill to protect his face. Waqar Younis bowled a bouncer at a great pace that hit his face and broke his nose, and blood splattered all over his face; the players and the officials advised that he retired hurt and went to the hospital; that was the moment of reckoning anybody else would have retired hurt, he was badly hurt, blood was streaming all over his face, the Pakistani bowlers were in incredible form, and they were hurting with their bowling. But Sachin stood his ground; in spite of all suggestions, he decided he wanted to play and continued playing with blood streaming and face hurting. The Pakistani bowlers and the players were intimidating, but Sachin refused to quit; he faced all attacks, persevered, scored 57, and saved that match. If he had quit, maybe he could have been dropped from the Indian Team, but he didn't, and that helped him continue playing the match; that incident also helped eliminate the fear of the fastest bowlers in the world: taking on a challenge made him a legend.

2. RAJNIKANT

Rajnikant is a big superstar in the Tamil Film Industry. Like most people who succeed by taking up a challenge, he also succeeded by taking up a challenge. Rajnikant's original name is Sivaji Rao Gaikwad. He belongs to a Marathi Hindu family. His ancestors hailed from a village near Pune, Maharashtra. His family had moved to Bangalore. He got a job as a Bus Conductor with Bangalore Transport Service, but the dull job was getting boring. To add excitement to his job, he acted, did some stunts, and entertained his passengers. They loved him, and many used to wait for his bus. However, his antics were not appreciated by his seniors because they felt that the job was getting trivialised. He faced a disciplinary charge and was asked to stop his acting and stunts at work. The job became boring, and his friend and coworker Raj Bahadur challenged him to be an actor. He took up the challenge and went to Chennai, which had an acting school. He enrolled in Adyar Film Institute and started learning acting. He couldn't speak Tamil, so he learnt to speak Tamil and took up odd jobs to support himself, including working as a coolie and loading rice bags into lorries. He did not even have the look of a Film Hero that was in vogue at that time, but that did not matter to him. Not having a steady income did not matter to him; not knowing the language to speak did not matter to him, but what mattered was that he had taken up the challenge. After struggling for a few years, he got some villain roles in which he excelled and soon became the unconventional hero in films, which succeeded because of his unique style and stunts. Rajnikant often said, *"En vazhi, thani vazhi,"* which meant, "I am unique, my ways are unique." This may also be true of you: *"You are unique; your ways would be unique."*

3. PATRICIA NARAYAN

Patricia Thomas, from Chennai, a city located in South India, was born into a conservative, devout Christian family. She fell in love and married Narayan, who belonged to a conservative Hindu Brahmin Family. Both families were against this inter-caste marriage and disowned them. They had to lead a life of extreme hardship and were blessed with two children. Narayan could not cope with the problems and challenges in life and turned into an alcoholic and drug addict. Patricia faced multiple challenges: no income, two kids to be taken care of, and a jobless drug addict for a husband who would torture her for money. There was no support from the family. She could endure the physical and mental abuse and insulate her kids from getting affected by the toxic environment, but there was a constant problem with money. She refused to get upset or angry; for her, it was a challenge. God was testing her; she would not fail God. She would not fail her children. She would find a solution.

She had her challenges as she did not have much education, and there was also a question of who would take care of her kids. She was a good cook and decided to start a small business selling food items in a cart. Fortunately, her mother discreetly gave her a small loan, and she started her business of selling South Indian delicacies of idli, vada, and dosa from that small cart at Marina Beach in Chennai. Her heart and soul would be in the batter that she prepared at home, and her passion came out in the quality of the food she made. Her children would study and play near her cart, and in service to society, she employed two handicapped persons. The authorities, seeing her struggle and determination against all odds, turned a blind eye to her illegal cart. The quality of her food, her low price, her passion, and her determination built up her reputation, and her story spread. Offices nearby gave her their canteen to run. Soon, she had canteens in many establishments in Chennai. Then, she started a chain of restaurants in Chennai called Sandeepa Group of Hotels and Restaurants. Her husband died of a drug overdose. Her daughter and son-in-law tragically died in a car accident. Patricia was shattered, but her devotion to work helped her to cope with her tragedies.

Patricia was awarded the Entrepreneur of the Year award in 2010 by the Federation of Indian Chamber of Commerce and Industry. She must be earning millions now, but that does not matter to her. What matters is the happiness she gives to others with the great food she serves and the difference that she could make in the lives of less fortunate, physically challenged fellow human beings that she is able to employ because of her business. Her grit, determination, passion, and perseverance overcame all adversity and are sources of inspiration. But what we may miss here is that her mind was engaged outside in her business. She did not brood, grieve, fret, or ruminate about the troubles in her life. She did not allow herself to get stressed. She took up the challenge. Being busy is the best way to manage stress.

4. ANN DUNHAM

One of the lesser-known stories of women who succeeded by taking up a challenge to resolve their problem is that of Ann Dunham, the mother of Barack Obama. As a student at Hawaii University, she fell in love with a student from Kenya, Barack Obama Senior. They got married and had a child – Barack Obama Junior. The senior Mr Obama abandoned the family and went back to Kenya. His tribe allowed him to have multiple marriages, and he had already been married before coming to America. Ann was left behind with a child to take care of. Then Cupid struck again; this time, she married a student from Indonesia, Lolo Soetoro. Ann followed her husband to Indonesia, had a daughter, Maya Soetoro, the half-sister of Barack Obama, got divorced, and came back to the United States. Then she said enough is enough; no more falling in love, getting married, having children, etc. She took up the challenge of making a difference in the world, helping women to be financially more secure. As a single mother with two children to take care of, she finished her degree, went on to finish her master's, did her PhD, and her research helped set up some of the biggest microfinance companies in the world in the developing economies, including Bangladesh and India. She educated her kids. Barack Obama studied at Harvard Law School and went on to become the 44th President of the United States. Her daughter, Maya Soetoro, earned her PhD from the University of Hawaii and continues the work started by her mother. Here, we need to add that although Ann took up the challenge, the credit also goes to her parents, Stanley and Madelyn Dunham, who had faith in their daughter and did not give up on her. Despite her missteps in life, they supported her in all her challenges. Maybe we might not have had Barack Obama as the President of the United States of America if his grandparents had given up on his mother because of her bad decisions early in her life. Ann Dunham took up the challenge.

5. **J.K ROWLING's Story Author of the Harry Potter Series of Books**

J. K Rowling, as a young student, was good at writing stories, while she was bad at mathematics, and her teacher felt that she would be duffer. She enjoyed being in the Brownies pack group, which hosted special events and parties as fairies, elves, gnomes, imps, etc, all magical figures. She loved to imagine herself in a magical world. Her father was a no-nonsense type of man, and the relationship between father and daughter was strained because the daughter was interested in the magic world instead of acquiring some real workplace skills. The early death of her mother was a great shock; she focused on her studies to escape the tension at home. She chose to study French and English Literature and took a course to be a secretary; the idea was that she could at least get work as a translator. She worked at temporary jobs but soon lost interest because her heart was not in that job; she lost her job, and she moved to Portugal to teach English to the Portuguese. She fell in love with a Portuguese man, married him and had a baby, but the marriage was falling apart, as her interest was In literature and writing novels; there were instances of domestic violence, and her husband threw her out of their home and with the help of police, she took possession of her daughter and her belongings which included early manuscript for Harry Potter Book. She moved back to England. Her father had remarried and did not want to take her in, so she moved to her sister's house. Not wanting to burden her sister, she moved to a mouse-ridden room where she could not even work. She sought government help and got 69 pounds a week to pay for her and her baby's expenses. She was very poor, and the need to take care of her child was causing great hardship, but she took up the challenge to write her novel no matter what. Multiple failures made her go through depression, and she confesses that she had thoughts to commit suicide multiple times, but her child and her determination to write her novel made her go through all hardship. She wrote on the train, she wrote in the café, she wrote in the garden, all the time rocking her kid on her lap. She used to write when the kid was sleeping. Her manuscript was rejected 12 times; even Bloomsbury Publisher initially threw the manuscript on the floor when he saw his eight-year-old daughter reading the magazine and was pleading with her father to allow her to continue to read well past her bedtime. Bloomsbury published that book, and to their and others' surprise, the book and the series became a big hit, popular all over the world; the series has sold more than 60 million copies worldwide, and many movies were made from that book, making J.K. Rowling a billion. She succeeded because she took up the challenge, focused on her work, and did not give up even in the worst situation.

6. JIM CARREY

Jim Carrey is known for his super successful films like The Mask, Dumb and Dumber, and The Truman Show, but many of us may not know about his early years of struggle and poverty and the 10 million cheque he issued to himself.

The story is that Carrey had issues with their studies because of his dyslexia condition, and his family was also struggling financially after his father lost his job. Although he tried to support his family by working in a Tyre Factory, he was physically unsuitable for the heavy labour work. He tried his hand at being a Stand-Up comic, which was his passion, but he was booed off the stage in his first attempt in Toronto. He did not want to go back to the factory as he did not have the qualifications for a good job, and Stand-Up Comedy was his passion. He made many attempts with mixed results; many times, he was told to go back, but he persisted. He moved to the United States and tried his luck in Los Angeles and Hollywood, but again, there was a mixed response.

One night, when he was booed out of a show, he went to the top of the Hollywood Hill and under the stars, he wrote a cheque to himself for 10 million dollars for acting services rendered and post-dated the cheque 10 years.

Showing that cheque to the stars, he called out to the universe, *"I take up the challenge, I will succeed, I will be paid 10 million for the acting services rendered."* Then, there was no looking back. He took up the challenge and did everything to scale up his craft. He persisted, persevered. He had taken up the challenge, and in less than 10 years, he was paid 10 million dollars for the acting service rendered for the movie Dumb and Dumber. This would seem incredible, but it is true. Once a mind is determined and takes up the challenge, it usually succeeds because of the powerful Artificial Intelligence System.

Some may call it manifestation, the law of attraction, the secret, etc., but there is a scientific theory for this and the Reticular Attention System in our brain goes in search of what you are seeking; it shuts off all information and prioritises the information you are looking for. This system is like a double-edged sword. If you are feeling negative, this system in your brain looks for more negativity. If you are afraid, it goes in search of more fear. When we are in negative situations, these negative emotions are automatically triggered, and they keep on growing because our neurons make automatic connections and create more disadvantages. But the same system can be used to our advantage. If you are in a negative situation but consider it a challenge, you refuse to be afraid, refuse to get anxious, get angry, get upset, refuse to get stressed, take up the situation as a challenge, and be human. That is, activate the qualities that make humans different from other animals: the ability of self-control, the ability not to give up, patience, tolerance, endurance, courage, perseverance, persistence, determination, discipline, grit, etc.

CHANDU CHAMPION – Mr. MURLIKANT RAJARAM PETKAR

Mr Murlikant Rajaram Petkar was born in a small village. It is believed that he picked a tiff with the village Headman's son, and to save his life, he had to run away from the village. While on the train, he met an army aspirant who accompanied him to the Army Recruitment Camp. His strength and mental fortitude impressed the recruiters, and he was selected for the army training. He got interested in boxing, but he had no formal training. He took up the challenge by watching the army boxers training; he challenged the champion in that camp; he got hit multiple times but persisted in being on his feet and got the camp champion down with a powerful knock when he got tired. He represented the army in many games. When the war broke out between India and Pakistan in 1965, he was called for army duty and was posted in the war zone when his camp was attacked by Pakistani planes spraying bullets. Nine bullets were pumped into him, and he suffered serious bullet injuries and was expected to die, but he was determined to live. The army doctors were able to remove eight bullets from his body, but they could not remove the

9th bullet because it had got lodged deep in his spine, disabling him from the waist down. Any attempt to remove that bullet may have killed him. He would never be able to do boxing, but he was determined to continue with the sport. It would have been difficult with his disability. He was challenged to swim, and he took up swimming with great earnestness in the Paralympics of 1968 held in Heidelberg; he won the first Gold Medal for India. He was determined that Paralympic sportspeople would also get the recognition they deserve, and he took up the challenge to bring the attention of the government to sports for the disabled. This ensured that the disabled also got the opportunity and recognition for their participation in sports. In 2018, he was awarded Padma Shri by the Indian Government. Mr Petkar succeeded against all odds because he took up the challenge.

ACCEPTANCE AND CHALLENGE

When individuals accept circumstances or perceive them as a challenge, different psychological and physiological response occur due to the way te brain and body interpret the situation.

1. **ACCEPTANCE OF CIRCUMSTANCES**

   Acceptance involves recognising and coming to terms with a situation without resistance. This state is associated with calmness and emotional regulation.

- **Reduced Stress:** Acceptance often lowers perceived stress because the individual stops fighting the reality of the situation.

- **Improved Emotional Balance:** Acceptance can lead to increased emotional stability and clarity of thought.

- **Increased Mindfulness:** Acceptance makes people more present-focused and less reactive.

- **Release of Negative Emotions:** Acceptance enables the release of negative emotions like anger, resentment, grudge, fear, etc.

- **Reduced Cortisol Levels:** Acceptance reduces the release of stress hormone cortisol, thus reducing stress and promoting relaxation.

- **Lower Heart Rate and Blood Pressure:** A calmer state leads to a steady heart rate and normalised blood pressure.

- **Improved Immune Function:** Stress reduction enhances immune system performance stress are triggered by sympathetic nervous system (SNS) , acceptance deactivates SNS and activates Parasympathetic Nervous system : The rest and digest system promotes relaxation, digestion and healing.

2. Viewing Circumstances as a Challenge

Seeing circumstances as challenges engages a proactive and adaptive response. It involves mobilising resources to address the situation, often associated with a sense of control and motivation.

- **Increased Motivation:** A challenge is seen as an opportunity for growth, fostering perseverance, persistence, grit and determination.

- **Positive Stress (Eustress):** Stress that is triggered in the body when circumstances are viewed as challenging is energising and improves focus.

- **Problem -Solving Mindset:** By viewing circumstances as challenge the focus shifts to finding solutions and achieving goals.

- **Moderate Increase in Cortisol and Adrenaline:** These hormones provide energy and focus, but unlike Distress in Eustress or Good Stress , the stress hormones remain within manageable levels just enough for the fire in you to drive you and not go out of control and get overwhelming.

- **Elevated Heart Rate and Blood Flow:** Viewing the circumstances as a challenge elevates the heart rate and blood flow, increases energy, and prepares the body for action.

- **Controlled Activation of Sympathetic Nervous System:** The "fight -or - flight" response is activated but there is ne fear, no anger or aggression. There is grit and determination.

Both the states are adaptive. Acceptance is beneficial for situations beyond control, while perceiving circumstances as a challenge is powerful when action can make difference. Balancing these responses based on the context is key to maintain well-being and resilience.

The situations in life where acceptance would be a better response could include situations like

Economic Downturn: like recession , job loss etc wherein acceptance would help individual focus on adapting to financial changes rather than resisting the situation.

Rejection or Failure: Recognising failure as part of growth helps in moving forward constructively.

Unchangeable Past: Acceptance and letting go of regrets or mistakes from the past can lead to emotional peace.

End of Relationship: Accepting that the relationship has ended fosters closure and emotional recovery.

Difference in Beliefs: Accepting diverse opinions or beliefs fosters understanding and reduces conflict.

Physical Limitations: Accepting physical or skill-based limitations enables individuals to work with their strengths.

Natural Disaster: Accepting what has happened, floods , earthquake, conflicts helps in focusing on recovery and rebuilding.

Chronic Illness: Accepting a long-term health condition allows for better management and adaptation to a new lifestyle.

Acceptance of Change: Adjusting or adapting to change can help reduce stress.

Ageing : Coming to terms with ageing, acceptance of wear and tear in the body , reduced energy, prevents unnecessary stress and fasters self-compassion.

Loss of Loved One: Grieving and accepting the loss helps in healing emotionally rather than resisting reality.

The Situations where viewing as a Challenge would be a better response include:

Career Growth: Seeing a demanding project or role as a challenge fosters personal and professional development.

Exams or Tests: Viewing these as opportunities to prove your abilities encourages preparation and focus.

Health Goals: Tackling weight loss, fitness, or overcoming addiction works better when seen as a challenge.

Financial Challenges: Taking on a challenge to increase income, reduces expenses, increase savings, budgeting, investments etc leads to financial stability.

Starting a Business: The initial challenge and obstacles in entrepreneurship are better handled with a challenge-oriented perspective.

Interpersonal Conflicts: Addressing conflicts as opportunities to improve communication and understanding fosters stronger relationships.

Setback and Failure: Viewing setbacks and failures as challenge, learning , opportunities to grow, builds grit and determination.

Sports or Competition: Competing with a mindset to improve and grow, taking it up as a challenge, enhances performance.

Social Change: Tackling systemic issues like inequality, community problem , climate change etc is most effective when approached as challenge.

Acceptance is the better response when the situation is **beyond our control** or requires emotional healing. **The challenge is the** better response when **action** or **effort** can lead to a positive change or growth. Balancing these responses as per the situation helps lead a more resilient and fulfilling life.

CONCLUSION

Stress is a defence mechanism, a survival instinct that activates when our mind perceives a situation as a threat. This fight-or-flight response, deeply rooted in the animal kingdom, prepares us to either confront the threat or escape from it. While this response once served humans well when survival was at stake, the nature of modern threats has fundamentally changed. Today, we are rarely faced with life-or-death situations; instead, we face challenges like competition, work pressure, financial struggles, relationship issues, etc. These are not physical threats but problems that require human responses - rationality, intelligence, and reasoning.

Yet, instinctively, humans continue to respond like animals. When confronted when confronted with challenges, Fear, Anxiety, Anger, Frustration, and Stress dominate our reactions. This misplaced response fails to resolve the problem and instead exacerbates the situation, harming our physical, mental and emotional well-being, as well as our relationships. Stress, while automatic, is not the solution; it is a detour. To fix a leaking roof, we must address the core issue, not merely patch up the damage.

The popular approach of managing stress through techniques like yoga, meditation, breathing exercises, and physical activity provides temporary relief. While these methods are helpful, they do not address the underlying issues triggering the stress. If the root cause remains unresolved, stress will persist, repeatedly overwhelming our system. Real change requires a shift in mindset and approach that addresses the challenges directly and allows one to respond like a human instead of reacting like an animal.

This book provides a comprehensive guide to achieving that shift. Through chapters like *Being Human, Stress Reduction for Millennials, How to Handle Emotions, Unique Concepts to Reduce Stress, Strategies to Reduce Stress. Techniques to Manage Stress.* This book offers practical solutions to identify and address core issues. It introduces unique concepts, powerful strategies, and inspiring stories of individuals who transformed their stress into success. By viewing problems as challenges and opportunities, they not only resolved their issues but also achieved extraordinary results in life.

The lessons in this book go beyond stress reduction. They empower you to tackle life's challenges head-on, reframe your perspective, and build a more fulfilling, successful, and happier life. Let this book be a guide to help you navigate modern problems with calm, clarity and purpose-allowing you to live not just stress-free but with a sense of meaning and achievement.

In the end, remember this; challenges are a part of life, but how you respond defines your journey. Choose to respond like human – with intelligence, resilience and mental strength.

Dear Readers,

Stress and loneliness have become silent epidemics of our time, affected countless lives and dimming the spark of humanity in people's hearts. As someone deeply committed to transforming lives. I invite you to join me on mission to reduce stress, foster connections, and help people reclaim their joy and inner peace.

Together, we can create a supportive community where individuals feel seen, heard, and understood. I am looking for passionate, compassionate individuals to join me as **Stress Support Guides.** In this role, you will:

1. **Be a Confidant and Guide**

    - Offer emotional support to individuals facing stress.

    - Listen without judgement and provide practical guidance to help them navigate life's challenges.

2. **Organise Stress Buster Meet-ups**

- Bring people together to share their stories and experiences.

- Facilitate activities and discussions that promote relaxation, laughter and camaraderie.

By becoming a Stress Support Guide, you won't just be helping others - you'll also grow as an individual, deepening your empathy and forging meaningful connections.

If you share this vision and are ready to make a difference, I encourage you to take the first step. Please reach out to me at stressresearchindia@gmail.com to learn more and join this transformative journey. Let's work together to create a world where no one has to face stress or loneliness alone.

Warm Regards
Guruprasad Shetty

AUTHOR BIO

Guruprasad Shetty, fondly known as Guru, has faced the crucible of stress for over four decades. With a career spanning senior managerial roles in top Indian companies and entrepreneurial ventures in specialised printing, garment manufacturing, retail and hospitality, he encountered the highs and lows of professional life.

A massive setback in one of his large ventures became a turning point, plunging him into chronic anxiety and stress that disrupted his health and relationships. Traditional methods of managing stress offered only temporary relief, failing to address the root cause. Determined to find a lasting solution, Guru embarked on a profound journey of self-discovery and research.

A lawyer by education, Guru approached stress with logic and reason. He discovered that stress stems from primal instincts designed for survival – the " fight or flight" response. While these instincts served early humans and animals in life-threatening situations, they no longer align with the challenges of modern life. Guru realised that humans often react to modern problems with outdated, animalistic responses, creating unnecessary harm to their physical, mental and emotional well-being.

His mission became clear: to help people replace stress-driven reactions with sensible, rational, intelligent, reasoned responses. By understanding stress as a bad habit rooted in our animal instincts, Guru advocates for cultivating the " good habit" of being human - sensible, composed and solution-focused. Today, Guruprasad Shetty shares his insights on empowering individuals to break free from the cycle of stress and lead healthier and more fulfilling lives. Through his journey, he inspires others to transform their challenges into opportunities for growth, resilience and humanity.

www.ingramcontent.com/pod-product-compliance
Lightning Source LLC
Chambersburg PA
CBHW021424150726
47989CB00001B/108